T0137521

DAD MOST High

Revolutionizing
Your Relationship
with God

Rigel J. Dawson

WESTBOW
PRESS®
A DIVISION OF THOMAS NELSON
& ZONDERVAN

WestBow Press books may be ordered through booksellers or by contacting:

WestBow Press
A Division of Thomas Nelson & Zondervan
1663 Liberty Drive
Bloomington, IN 47403
www.westbowpress.com
1 (866) 928-1240

ISBN: 978-1-9736-7900-4 (sc)
ISBN: 978-1-9736-7901-1 (hc)
ISBN: 978-1-9736-7899-1 (e)

Library of Congress Control Number: 2019918211

Print information available on the last page.

WestBow Press rev. date: 12/2/2019

Dedicated to my dad
Thornton J. Dawson
a great father & a great man

Contents

Acknowledgements

I want to give a special thanks to my wonderful mother, Laura, whose heart is full of compassion and love. I am eternally grateful for your encouragement and for all that you have done to support me in the pursuit of my dreams.

To my beautiful wife, Qiana, I say, "Thank you, thank you, thank you!" You hold me up and push me forward. Thank you for your patient, gracious, and understanding spirit. You are my virtuous woman!

I have to give a shout out to my amazing children, Rylan and Roman! You fill my days with light and laughter. It is my greatest joy in life to be your dad, and I hope that I can always be the one you want and need. I couldn't have written this book if God had not blessed me with you.

I must give a special acknowledgement to the Family of Faith church, which I have the great honor of serving. Thank you so much for letting me be your preacher! This book was born out of a sermon series that the Lord placed on my heart and you were gracious enough to let me proclaim to you. I truly appreciate all of the love and support you give me.

I have to also express deep gratitude to all the mentors who have poured into me throughout the years of my kingdom service, and even before it began. There is no way to repay the contributions you have made to my ministry or to fully express how you helped position me to walk in my purpose. I can only hope to make you proud by moving faithfully in my calling. Know that my success is part of your legacy.

Finally, I give all glory to Abba God for His longsuffering and His love. Whatever ability I have to teach and encourage through the gift of writing is truly His grace at work in my life. I hope and pray that He is magnified throughout the pages of this book and that someone will be drawn closer to Him because He led me to write it.

1

A Question of Identity

As many things do, this book begins with a great song. It's not a traditional church hymn or even a modern praise and worship ballad. This song has nothing to do with church, and there's nothing spiritual about the lyrics, per se. But, man, what a great song!

Back in the '70s, Bill Withers asked an important question in musical form. The song is called "Who Is He (And What Is He to You)." If you've never heard it, do yourself a favor and go YouTube it or something.

You're welcome.

Of course, Bill was giving melodic voice to his jealous suspicions. He was checking his girlfriend over the telling looks she was getting from another man. But the circumstances of the question aren't what I want you to focus on right now; I want you to focus on the question itself.

See, the question reminds us of a profound truth that relates to our existence as human beings: identity is everything.

When you get pulled over, the first thing the officer wants to know is who you are. The first question people ask when they meet you is what your name is, and the second question they ask is what you do, just another way of finding out who you are and how you define yourself.

Identity, or rather our understanding of it, frames our decisions and forms our motivations. Who we think we are determines what we do and how we do it and even *why* we do it. Think about how many times you've heard someone who was asked why they did something respond by saying, "That's just who I am."

When it comes to our spiritual lives, identity is everything. I hope you know by now that you can't really do what you're supposed to do until you know who you are. And as a believer, your identity is tied to the identity of your God. One of the first things scripture reveals to us about our nature as human beings is that we were created in the image of the One who created us.

So it comes down to this: you don't know who *you* are until you know who *He* is.

These questions determine the direction of your entire spiritual walk. If He's mostly Master, and in relation to that, you see yourself mostly as a servant, then that understanding of identity dictates how you move with Him. I'm guessing there's a lot of fear in your Christian walk, a lot of worry about whether you're being good enough or doing enough of the right things.

If He's mostly King or Lord to you, and you see yourself as merely a subject or a supplicant, you probably struggle with feelings of emptiness and insignificance even while you worship and work religiously. You carefully dot all your t's and cross all your i's but still don't seem to really be getting anywhere in your spiritual life.

Because of the way you've been taught to see God, you may even struggle at times with whether or not you're really saved. You might be on the proverbial rollercoaster of emotions in regard to your eternal life. One day you're riding high at the apex of confidence and joy, and the next day you've bottomed out in doubt and despair!

Now, don't get me wrong. I'm not saying He's *not* Master and King and Lord. He's all that and more! When He introduced Himself to Moses in Exodus 3:14, He simply said, "I AM WHO I AM." No single name or label would have been sufficient to capture the sum of His being. He just *is*. He's whatever you need.

Are you sick? He's Healer.

Are you lost? He's Shepherd.

Are you poor? He's Provider.

Are you lonely? He's Love.

And, yes, He's most assuredly Master, King, and Lord. The list goes on and on. Whatever you need Him to be, He's that and then some.

You could write volumes on each of those roles God plays in our lives, but the point of *this* book is that we often miss one of the most important aspects of God's identity. And in missing it, we also end up missing out on the fullness of our relationship with Him.

See, I believe that what God wants to be to us—far more than He wants to be King or Master—is *Father*. When you really learn to see God first and foremost as your Abba, it drastically changes how you relate to Him.

It blows open the doors on an incredibly powerful prayer life that isn't bound by form and formality!

It imparts an amazing sense of spiritual security and frees you from chasing what you already have!

It fills you to overflowing with an unshakeable joy that rests firmly on a foundation of unconditional love!

When you learn to see God as your Father, you can no longer see yourself as just a servant, only a subject, or merely a supplicant. You see yourself as a *son*, and that changes everything. So let's take what I hope will be an enlightening and encouraging journey together, and it starts with the question from the song: who is He and what is He to you?

Dear Abba,

I praise you as the multi-tasking God that you are! I thank you for perfectly filling so many different roles and for satisfying so many different needs and desires in my life. You are my Provider. You are my Shepherd. You are my Master. You are my Healer. You are my Counselor. You are my King.

I pray that you'll continue to reveal yourself to me. Show me who you are to me, and show me who I am to you. Lead me to an ever-deepening understanding as you manifest your love for me on all these different levels.

Most of all, I pray today that you will show me what it means to have you as my Father. Open my eyes to the blessings of being not just your servant but your child, and teach me how to walk in the fullness of this wonderful relationship. In the saving name of Jesus, amen!

2

Back to the Beginning

Speaking of songs, you've probably heard one or two about how we were made to worship, right? There are a few nice ones out there. Not to take anything away from the musicians who've made some really beautiful music, but they're not exactly telling the truth.

It sounds good and it seems to make sense on the surface, but you and I were *not* made to worship God.

First of all, think about the implications of that statement. What does it say about God that He created an entire race of beings for the sole purpose of worshipping Him? Kinda makes Him sound like a lonely, narcissistic egomaniac!

If God is as all-good and all-loving as the scriptures tell us He is, then it doesn't add up that He would be so vain as to make humanity just to have someone to bow down to Him and give Him offerings and tell Him how awesome He is. That doesn't sound like love; that sounds like pride. If God had made you and me to worship Him, then that would make Him a taker and that would go against His nature. Love doesn't take; it gives. God is love, and that makes Him the ultimate Giver.

Secondly (and more importantly), think about what the Bible does and doesn't say. The Bible tells us that God is worthy of our worship. The Bible tells us that God desires and delights in our true spiritual worship. The Bible encourages, even commands, us to worship God. But the Bible doesn't tell us that we were *made* to worship God.

I've seen verses like Psalm 95:6 and Isaiah 43:7 cited as proof that we were. But you have to ignore the context and stretch the Word to make those passages say that we were created to worship. Yes, the psalmist invites and encourages us to bow down to our Maker, but that's not the same thing as saying God *made* us to worship Him. He's just giving us one more reason (among several in that psalm) why He's worthy.

In Isaiah, God was talking about restoring his covenant people, Israel. They were the nation He had made for His glory. He's not talking about why He created humankind. And there's far more to God's glory than just worshipping Him anyway.

The Bible doesn't say we were created to worship.

The truth is, man wasn't made to worship God; he was made to *walk* with God. That's a huge difference. When you grasp that, it drastically shifts how you see God and how you see yourself in relation to God.

Go back and study the first few chapters of Genesis again. Do you notice what's glaringly absent from those chapters in contrast to what we see all throughout the rest of the Old Testament?

Worship.

Nowhere in there do we see Adam offering any sacrifices to God in the garden. There's not a single mention of an altar. There's no blueprint for a temple. There's no record of God prescribing any acts of reverence or demanding any offerings.

See, worship didn't come into the picture until we messed up the walk. It wasn't until after the Fall of man that we see offerings demanded and sacrifices commanded.

With sin now at work in our hearts and lives, we needed worship to help us remain reverent and obedient.

With pride now pushing us to push back against our Creator, we needed worship to help us remember our place.

With a weight of condemnation hanging over us, we needed worship to remind us that redemption has a price and to point us to the One who would eventually pay that price in full.

But worship isn't really what our Father wanted from us.

What we actually see in the very beginning is the great God of the entire universe hanging out with the man and woman He created in a paradise made just for them! That's not religion—that's relationship. And relationship with God is where humankind *began*, not where we eventually arrived.

We sometimes make the mistake of presenting the work of Jesus as setting humanity free from religion, fulfilling the Mosaic Law and finally bringing us into relationship with God for the first time. That's not accurate. We were already in relationship with God. Religion only came into the picture when we ruined the relationship.

The truth is that Jesus came to bring us *back* into relationship with God. His death and resurrection were the culmination of a restorative ministry. Jesus didn't come to *introduce* humanity to God; He came to *reconcile* humanity to God! In other words, He came to put things back the way they were in the beginning.

So go back to the beginning. Picture what was happening. God wasn't sitting on a throne waiting to be served. He wasn't some aloof deity with His nose stuck in the air, scowling at the puny humans scurrying around in the dirt. He was *with* Adam and Eve, *walking* with them every day.

Have you ever thought about that? When God came looking for them on that fateful day after they ate the fruit, I'm convinced that wasn't the first time He had done so. Remember, He was walking in the garden and He was *looking* for them. God expected to find them that day just like He had every other day. I get the impression that He was ready for their evening stroll! And they would have taken it together that day like they had every other day if sin didn't have the man and woman hiding from their Maker. Now they were guilty and ashamed and unable to enjoy His presence the way they always had before.

But back to that walk. I wonder what they talked about each day. Was God giving Adam gardening tips? Were they laughing at inside jokes? Was He confiding deep spiritual truth to them? Maybe all of the above. The point is that before the separation of sin, God was regularly coming down and communing with man in the garden.

And that's exactly how He meant it to be!

In the beginning, God was with man. That's what Jesus came to give us back. It's no wonder He's called Emmanuel. He put on flesh and came down here to be God With Us. Even though He knew this time He wouldn't be walking with us in paradise—far from it—He came and walked with us anyway.

Our Emmanuel talked with us and shared His heart with us. He worked with us and cried with us. He laughed with us and loved with us. He Himself went through the same storms that we go through. He taught us and corrected us and encouraged us face to face. He bled with us. He bled *for* us.

You need to know that you have a personally present God who created you, not so that He would have someone to worship Him, but so that He would have someone to walk with Him. That's why you were made.

Dear Abba,

I thank you for opening my eyes and helping me to see more clearly why you made me. You are worthy of my worship, and I freely give it to you. But I rejoice in the knowledge that you actually created me to walk with you! My heart soars to think that what you really want is to have an intimate fellowship with me, that someone like you wants to have a close personal connection with someone like me! I'm so small and unworthy and insignificant compared to you. I'm nothing, but *you* want to walk with *me*! That's almost too much for me to comprehend.

I pray that you'll continue to free me from the bondage of seeing my Christianity as a religion and release me into the joy and freedom and peace of seeing it as a relationship with you. Thank you for your Son Jesus who came to walk with us and bring us back into fellowship with you. Teach me what that means and let me fully embrace the power of that fellowship in my life. In His wonderful name, amen!

3

Made for Walking

Okay, so I know somebody reading this may be struggling with it. The idea that we were made to worship God may have been drummed into you, and it's always hard to, in the words of Master Yoda, "unlearn what you have learned." But it's necessary. Getting your mind wrapped around the idea that you were actually made to walk with God may take some time, but embracing that truth is going to bless you immensely. Let me help you with some more scriptural evidence.

Consider this: one of only two people in the Bible described as not having experienced a natural death is Enoch. We have next to nothing regarding the details of his life. We know he was the son of Jared. We know he lived for 365 years. We know he named his son Methuselah for some reason. And that's pretty much it.

Oh, except for the fact that, one day, Enoch just wasn't there anymore because God took him away! No deathbed goodbyes. No funeral services. No cremation or burial. He bypassed all of that. God just took him away! What an incredible honor! What an astounding testimony! What an awesome epitaph for his monument: He was no more because God took him.

And the reason He took him? Because Enoch walked with God! That's how highly God values relationship with His creation.

Enoch was one guy who got it right. Connection. Intimate fellowship. Dare I say, *friendship*? And because he got it right, God was so delighted with Enoch that He gave him his own personal rapture!

Now, we don't know fully and exactly what it means that Enoch walked with God because the scriptures don't give us the specifics of his life. Much of what we'd come up with if we tried to describe it would only be speculation. But the Word does tell us enough about walking with someone that we can say a few things about Enoch's life with certainty.

We can definitely say that Enoch trusted God. For the Lord to be so deeply pleased with the man, there must have been plenty of the one thing He wants most from all of us—faith. Psalm 23 reminds us that our Shepherd walks with us even through the valley of the shadow of death. And because He's right there beside us every step of the way, we don't need to fear any evil thing that crosses our path.

I believe that Enoch had so much faith that he trusted God implicitly. I believe that, even at the lowest points of his life, he found peace and comfort in the unwavering presence of the Lord. Walking with God means going wherever He leads, moving with Him in absolute confidence that, as long as He's with you, everything's going to be alright.

We can also say for certain that Enoch agreed with God. One of the rhetorical questions God asked in Amos 3:3 was, "Do two walk together, unless they have agreed to meet?" Obviously not! There must be mutual consent. There has to be a shared intent to move together toward the same destination. Now, when you're walking with God, you don't set the agenda; you get with His program! Even the Greek word for "confess" literally means to say the same thing, to agree with what someone else has already said.

Enoch must have moved constantly in submissive consent to the will of the Lord. And even when he went astray—as we all do—he acknowledged it and came back to the right way right away. Walking with God means living a life that says, "Amen!" whenever He speaks His wisdom and truth.

And I think we can definitely say that Enoch communed with God. The picture of the two disciples walking the road to Emmaus after Jesus' resurrection has always stood out to me. You can find it in Luke 24. These two men headed to the same town were talking while they were walking. It was a time of confusion and fear, and they were reasoning together, maybe even debating back and forth as they wrestled in their minds over what was happening. They were sharing thoughts and trading ideas. These two were opening their hearts to each other, exposing their disappointments and anxieties as they tried to make sense of everything that had taken place.

I believe that Enoch conversed with God and reasoned together with God. Maybe he even argued with God! I believe that he sought the Lord diligently, both listening to Him and talking to Him, struggling to know his Maker more deeply and gain a better grasp of His ways. Walking with God means being a fervent follower, always craving His divine presence and always striving to fathom the unfathomable.

So the point is this—Enoch walked with God. Whatever else that meant, however that looked, Enoch walked with God. And *that's* what God wanted. That's what God rewarded. Not just worship. Not sacrifices offered or service rendered.

What pleased God most, what He chose to honor in such a unique and amazing way at the end of Enoch's earthly journey was the fact that Enoch chose to move in close companionship with Him. And in doing so, Enoch fulfilled the very purpose for which he was created.

Dear Abba,

I pray for a deeper understanding of my purpose. Help me to grasp the truth of your desire, above all else, for me to walk with you. Keep setting me free from any wrong ideas about why you put me here, and don't let me slip back into bondage once you've liberated me. Help me to keep the most important aspect of my nature at the center of my identity—that I am your child and you made me to live in fellowship with you!

Thank you for the amazing testimony of a man like Enoch who shows us where your heart for us really is. Help me to want that same walk with you. Grow in me a strong passion to please you as he did, a deep longing to find favor in your eyes!

Help me to trust you no matter how rough the road gets. Help me to submit more fully to your will for my life, even when I don't understand it. And help me to connect with you deeply and personally, growing every day in my appreciation of who you are to me and who I am to you. In Jesus' name, amen!

4

A Father's Pain

I love the way the genealogy of Jesus ends in Luke 3. It traces His earthly father Joseph's lineage all the way back to the beginning of creation. Joseph, who was the son of Heli... David, who was the son of Jesse...Isaac, who was the son of Abraham...Shem, who was the son of Noah, and so on. All the way back to the very first man, Adam, who was the son of God.

Adam was the son of God! He wasn't the *servant* of God or the *worshipper* of God. The Spirit calls him the *son* of God. That's how God saw Adam. That's how He treated him. That's what God made Adam to be. His very own offspring. A chip off the old block. A precious child, carefully and lovingly made in His own image.

I think our misconceptions of God lead us to assume that judgment is easy for Him. We see Him as a cold-hearted dictator, someone for whom doling out punishment is no big deal. We sometimes picture Him stoically sealing up the garden and sending Adam and Eve away with no emotion or pain. That doesn't ring true when you really get to know God.

When you come to see your Father for who He is, you realize that His heart *had* to be breaking. Our sin was deeply devastating to Him. It was personally and immensely painful.

Man lost paradise, but God did too.

Imagine the Father's hurt when He couldn't walk with His children anymore. If you're a parent who's lost a child that you got to love for a season, you may know what that feels like. My wife and I suffered two miscarriages, and that was the worst kind of pain for us. We never even got to nurture those babies or watch them grow, but losing them still hurt like nothing I've ever felt.

So I can't imagine losing my two-year-old son or burying my daughter at age five. I can't imagine having the chance to live with and love on a baby for months or years and then losing that child. There can't possibly be any greater feeling of hurt and loss in this life.

Maybe you're a military mom or dad who's had to be away for long stretches of time. Or the victim of some other circumstance that kept you separated from your kids for longer than you wanted to be. If so, you know that desperate, aching desire to hold your baby or to pick her up from school or to take him to the park to play, but you just couldn't. No matter how badly you wanted to, you just couldn't. Your heart broke a little bit every night you weren't there to tuck them in.

God the Father had the chance to walk with His children. He got to see Adam get up off the ground and take his first tentative steps. He got to bless His son with the amazing gift called "woman." (It must have been like watching our kids on Christmas morning!) He got to see Eve open her eyes for the first time and marvel at the beauty that surrounded her in that perfect, pristine world.

God got to talk with His son and daughter. He got to hear their voices and listen to their laughter. He got to be face to face with His offspring and enjoy every little nuance of their burgeoning personalities. He got to experience them savoring for the first time all the incredible tastes and smells of the garden that He gave them.

And then one day, all of that came to an end. Because of the disastrous circumstance of sin, the Father's fellowship with His children was abruptly ripped away from Him. No matter how badly He wanted to, He couldn't be with His children anymore.

That *had* to hurt.

By the way, if you've ever wrestled with questions about the wrath of God, if you've ever wondered how a good God could show His anger in the ways He has, there's your answer. See, that's why God hates sin as much as He does. It's not because He likes making rules and enforcing them. Sin is detestable to Him because it's the enemy that stands between Him and what He loves most—*you.*

So God has to hate sin. He must warn us against it and He has no choice but to punish it. Love demands that He does. God hates sin so much because He loves sinners so much!

For a father who loves his children, the worst possible pain is not being able to be with them. It will bring him to tears. He may not let you *see* him cry, but trust me when I tell you that the tears will flow. It will infuriate him, and whoever or whatever is keeping him from his kids will likely bear the brunt of his rage, even if that's their mother. It will crush him with sorrow, maybe even drive him to a dangerous place of despondency and depression. If a man has a heart, being kept from the children he cherishes will break it.

God was the first Father ever. And if we feel that way as parents, imagine how He feels when He can't be with His babies.

Dear Abba,

Thank you for helping me see how my sin affects you. Give me a heart of godly sorrow for my wrongs and transgressions. Make sin more and more distasteful to me. Keep me from getting comfortable with it or from being casual about its presence in my life. Please cleanse my heart and renew a righteous spirit within me.

I pray that you'll take away any false thoughts about you that the enemy would have me hold on to. Keep me from falling back into the belief that punishment is easy for you or that you take pleasure in it. I know that you don't revel in wrath, but I also know that your love and justice demands it.

Father, I praise you today for your nurturing heart! I see in your Word the great care that you showed your first children and I rejoice in the knowledge that you still care for your children now with that same loving heart. You haven't changed and you never will. Keep me close to you and cover me with your grace. In the amazing name of Jesus, amen!

5

Just Because You Are

Many of you will know this from experience, either from *having* good parents or from *being* good parents (or both). Some of you may not have had either experience, so you may not fully grasp this, and that's okay. Either way, you need to know that mothers and fathers—at least those in their right mind and spirit—love their children unconditionally.

This doesn't mean that our feelings and our favor don't wax and wane depending on their behavior and performance. There are times when we're extra proud and times when we're sorely disappointed. But a real parent's love doesn't depend on what his or her child does or doesn't do. It's constant. It's steady. And it's always there, even before the child does anything, good or bad.

See, good parents don't love their children because their children are *good*; they just love their children because they *are*. Moms and dads love their kids for no other reason than the fact that they exist! My daughter didn't have to do anything to earn my love. My son didn't have to pass any tests or perform to a certain standard before I started loving him.

In fact, when they were babies, our children *couldn't* do anything for us; we had to do everything for them. We had to feed them, burp them, dress them, soothe them, wipe them, change them, and carry them everywhere. Talk about a one-sided relationship! But you know what? We loved them like crazy even though they contributed nothing to the household.

My wife and I loved our children the moment they were born just because they existed and they were little versions of us. In fact, we loved them *before* they even drew their first breaths. Like many fathers out there, I was instantly in love with my daughter and my son the moment my wife told me she was pregnant each time.

For the nine months they were baking in her belly, I was daydreaming about their lives and praying for their health and well-being. I was painstakingly painting their rooms and talking to them and playing The Godfather and Star Wars soundtracks for them in the womb. (I mixed in some Mozart, too.) I hadn't even laid eyes on them yet, but from the second I knew they had been conceived, those little people became my entire world.

And just like there was nothing our children could do to make us *start* loving them, there's nothing they can do to make us *stop* loving them. Sometimes they disobey me and their mother. Sometimes they argue and fight with each other. Sometimes they do things they know are wrong, and I know they know they're wrong! There are times when they anger and frustrate and disappoint us, and times when they have to be punished.

But none of it changes our love for them.

This is how you need to see your spiritual Father. You did nothing to earn your Father's love, and there's nothing you can do to lose it. He loves you because you exist and you're His. He has always loved you and He always will. Even when you've completely blown it, He has never ceased loving you.

If you don't already hold that truth deep in your spirit, you need to get it there and keep it there! Say it out loud every day several times a day. Even if you struggle to believe it at first, say it anyway and keep saying it: "My Abba is love! And He loves me just because I am! I don't have to be good enough to get His love; I already have it!"

Many of us have been beaten down with an unbiblical performance-based brand of Christianity. This skewed indoctrination has warped our thinking and made us believe that we've got to be good enough to get love from God. Even if it's not explicitly stated, much of our preaching and teaching implies that we need to earn His acceptance. The early church had to deal with variations of that off-key theme, and it's been heard in various forms throughout history up until today.

And we believe that, even if we do somehow manage to put together a good enough religious resume to get God to love us, it's a tenuous situation at best. Our mischaracterization of God makes us feel like He accepts us, but only reluctantly. We feel like He tentatively lets us in, but we're just one misstep away from being cast out all over again. That broken perception makes us think we're always on shaky ground, never truly stable in our relationship with Him.

Sadly, in many believers' minds, God's default setting is disapproval. They see Him sitting on His throne with crossed arms and a skeptical scowl, cynically waiting to see what we've got. We mistakenly believe that because we're so bad and He's so good, we have to work really hard at being good, and then maybe, just maybe He'll slowly start to warm up to us after we stack enough brownie points to prove to Him that we're not so bad after all.

God's default setting is love. He doesn't just give love; He *is* love, as 1 John 4:8 tells us. That's His very nature, His true essence. It's the core of who He is.

Does sin anger Him? Certainly. Does He hate the ungodly and wicked things that separate us from Him? Absolutely. But God's natural countenance is not a disappointed frown or a hateful glare. It's a loving gaze, a longing look of compassion for the children He created in His image and called "very good," the precious living souls that He cherishes deeply.

Tragically, many of us are going through life with no expectation of love from God. We've been conditioned to think it's conditional. And deep down, we know we can't meet the conditions. We know we're not that good. We know we struggle with sin. We know we fall far short of His perfection. And so we trudge through our spiritual lives knowing better than to expect love and approval, just hoping that somehow our good outweighs our bad and tips the scale of God's grudging acceptance in our favor.

But when you embrace the fact that your Father is love, you start to expect love from Him. You know you're loved even when you know you haven't been all that lovable. You start looking for good things. You anticipate His favor. You begin to believe Him for blessings because you know that He *wants* to bless you!

And because you know you're already loved, it makes you want to love Him all the more by living obediently to His will for your life. You start working *from* God's love, not *for* it.

Dear Abba,

I praise you today for your loving nature. I thank you that none of my mistakes or failures change how you choose to relate to me. I thank you that you love me through all of my sin and selfishness, through all of my weakness and my wickedness.

Teach me to expect love and grace from you, not because *I'm* so good, but because *you* are. I pray that you'll finish freeing me from the false belief that I need to be good enough to gain your love, that I somehow have to earn it from you. I ask you to completely uproot that lie from my spirit and replace it with the perfect peace of knowing that you have always loved me and that you always will.

Thank you for not casting me aside. Thank you for not writing me off. And thank you for not loving me the way I have "loved" so many people in my life. Show me how to do better and to give to others what you have given to me. In Jesus' perfect name, amen!

6

You Don't Have To Get What You've Already Got

How you're loved determines how you live. If you're loved conditionally, then you're always working for it. You never stop jumping through hoops. You never get to take a break from trying to prove yourself. You never get to rest from trying to perform well enough to please the one whose love you're chasing. When you mess up in that person's eyes, you're wracked with shame and desperate for a chance to make it up to them and get back in their good graces.

Can I say this while we're on the subject? If you're in a relationship like this with someone, you need to know that what you have is *not* real love. The enemy may have twisted your thinking and made you believe that it is, but it's not.

Real love doesn't withhold care and affection until you meet certain standards. It doesn't belittle and shame you when you don't get it right. Real love doesn't dangle its goodness just out of your reach and force you to go a little faster, stretch a little farther, or try a little harder to obtain it. It doesn't make you prove your worthiness over and over again.

Real love accepts you for who you are while encouraging you to become your best self. Real love is patient and kind and generous and uplifting. If that's not what you have with a person, either stand up for yourself and start working to change the dynamic of the relationship or leave that relationship behind you where it belongs.

When you're loved unconditionally by someone, you don't feel the pressure to perform for them. There's no glaring spotlight on your every word and deed, no scrutinizing gaze or judgmental sneer to constantly contend with. There's no emotional blackmail, no manipulation, no threats to withhold what it has to give until you've given what it wants.

Unconditional love is just there. All the time. It's steady and safe and comfortable. You don't have to work for it.

And when you don't have to work *for* love, you start to work *from* love. That work is always more energetic, more joyful, and more effective.

At a certain point in my life, something shifted in my relationship with my parents. Somewhere along the way I realized how good I had it. Two parents in the home. A dad who never complained while he worked hard to give us a better life than he had, all the while modeling good morals and strong character. A mom who worked out of the home and in the home, a great teacher and encourager who made sure my brother and I had good experiences and wonderful memories.

When it sunk in how blessed I was—how *loved* I was—chores weren't a chore anymore. I found that I (kinda) *wanted* to clean the bathroom, vacuum the floor, and pick up after myself. I *wanted* to kick in for "rent" and buy my mom and dad nice gifts when I got older and started making some money of my own. It wasn't a burden; I enjoyed doing for my parents because my parents had done so much for me.

I loved them because they first loved me.

Working *for* love is hard. It's painful, soul-crushing drudgery that's hardly ever rewarded. It drains your energy and slowly breaks your heart. It erodes your self-esteem and leaves you feeling worthless.

Working *from* love is easy. It's exciting and fun. It ignites your spirit and energizes your creativity. There's a huge difference between wanting to please someone who's already shown beyond a shadow of a doubt that they love you, and feeling like you have to please someone in order to make them love you. One is desire; the other is duty. One is seen as an opportunity, the other as an obligation.

Jesus said, "Come to me, all who labor and are heavy laden, and I will give you rest. Take my yoke upon you, and learn from me, for I am gentle and lowly in heart, and you will find rest for your souls" (Matthew 11:28–29).

The Teacher was talking to everyone who had been laboring under the Mosaic Law, striving to be righteous by keeping its rules and regulations. He was speaking to all the people who were wearing themselves out struggling to be good enough to get God's approval. He was talking to everyone who was languishing under the heavy load of legalism, trying to live up to man-made standards of righteousness and piety.

The Teacher was talking to all of us.

Now, make no mistake—Jesus didn't say there was no work to be done. He simply said that when we come to accept Him as the Truth, the nature of our work and the motivation for it changes drastically. He still says there's a yoke to wear, but it's *His* yoke and it's one that's easy to wear. He tells us His burden is light. In Him, we still work, but we've swapped an impossibly heavy load for one that's manageable.

This load doesn't break you down—it actually builds you up as you carry it.

Jesus was telling us that working *from* God's love is infinitely easier and lighter than working *for* it. Your service to Him ceases to be drudgery—it becomes joy. You *want* to work, you *long* to minister, you *crave* to serve because you revel in the amazing love that's already been given to you.

So know that your Father already loves you. He loved you before you loved you. He loved you before you loved Him. He already loves you as much as He *can* love you, and there's nothing you can do to make Him stop loving you. When you get that in your heart, the whole spirit of your walk with God will change.

Dear Abba,

I'm so grateful for a love that I can rest in. Thank you for a love that's constant and steady, one that I don't have to replenish by my performance. Help me to get free and to stay free from the trap of thinking that I have to work for your love.

Help me remember that whatever I do for you is just a chance to love you back for the unchanging, unconditional love you've already given to me. Release me to rejoice again in my service to you and to others. Let me not simply see it as a difficult duty that I have to perform, but as a privilege and a pleasure. I pray that your amazing love will reignite my passion for ministry and revive my joy for your kingdom work.

Please forgive me for the times in my life when I've made people work for my affection and approval. I pray for a heart of generosity and grace in my relationships with others. Teach me to freely give encouragement, kindness, and admiration to my family and friends, not waiting for anything up front or expecting anything in return. Teach me to be like you. In Jesus' name, amen!

7

Seriously... You've Already Got It!

I don't know about you, but I used to struggle with Philippians 2:12. That's where Paul talks about working out your salvation. Growing up, I always heard that we're saved by grace. But I also always heard this verse quoted as proof that if you didn't stay busy, busy, busy for the Lord, you might not make it into heaven. You had to keep working for your salvation.

But it doesn't say that at all. It says, "work *out*," not "work *for*."

The Greek word Paul used would have been very meaningful to people living in a farming culture. It has to do with working a field to get the most produce from it, putting in the effort to get the optimal harvest. The farmer already owns the field; he's not working to obtain it. And even if he doesn't do anything, the field is probably going to yield something. The earth is going to do what it does; nature's just good that way. *Something's* going to grow.

But how much *more* will the farmer get if he plows and plants and weeds and waters? What will the increase be if he's smart about letting parts of his land lie fallow for a time? What will he gain if he invests in oxen and equipment, if he gets up early and stays up late working in his field?

Exactly!

Your field is your salvation, and you already have it. It was a gift of God's grace that you received by believing in Him. It's yours by faith, not by works. Even if you don't do much of anything after you're saved, something good is still coming out of you accepting Christ. You're still going to heaven by the grace of God through Jesus.

But how much *more* will you get out of your salvation if you work it?!?

How many more people can get what you've got if you faithfully serve? How many lives can be changed for the better? How many others can be led to receive that same saving grace? Diligent ministry doesn't save you, but how much more glory does God get from saved people who minister diligently than from those who don't?

Paul is saying that since you've already got it, you should work hard to get the most out of your salvation for God, for others, and for yourself.

And don't let the "fear and trembling" part in that verse throw you. Paul's not saying that we should cower in dread of God and constantly worry about whether we're doing enough to please the awful taskmaster we serve. He's not saying we need to live life on edge, never quite sure if we're being good enough to get to heaven.

That's what I always took from the way I heard this passage taught growing up. Then I learned that the phrase "fear and trembling" is a Hebraism. It's a common expression that the Jewish people used to speak of the awe they had for God, in both a negative and a positive sense.

Yes, there's an element of terror when you contemplate the wrath of God against sin, but that's not even a thing anymore for those of us who are in Christ. For us, Paul reminds, there is no condemnation (Romans 8:1). And if there's no condemnation, then there's really nothing to fear.

For us, the fear and trembling is not quaking in fright over God's wrath but, rather, being deeply moved by the wonder of His love and grace. Psalm 2:11 connects fear and trembling with rejoicing! Sometimes something is so *awesome* that it shakes you just as much as the thing that's *awful*.

If your Christian walk is one of mortal dread, you're doing it all wrong. If you're constantly living in fear of God's punishment or you're "trying not to go to hell," you've kinda missed the point. Either you haven't really repented of a sinful life or you don't really grasp that whole "no condemnation" thing Paul was talking about.

God doesn't want us to be scared of Him.

Yes, He wants us to hold Him in reverence and have a healthy fear of His wrath against sin. That's right and that's reasonable! We *should* be afraid of the manifestations of God's anger against things that are wicked and wrong. But we shouldn't be *walking* in fear of His anger if we've been delivered from the things that make Him angry.

Think about it from our human perspective—good parents don't want to scare their children. (Remember, we're talking about those in their right minds.) Of course we want our children to respect us. Yes, we absolutely want our children to carry a healthy fear of the consequences of bad behavior.

But we don't want our children to be *scared* of us. We don't want them to run and hide when they hear us coming. We never want them to break out in tears when we enter the room or flinch when we move in their direction.

Neither does God.

We want our children to run and jump into our arms when we get home! We want them to *want* to be around us. We want them to feel safe and comfortable and protected when we're with them. And we want them to eventually do right, not just because they fear what will happen if they do wrong, but because they trust our teaching and example, because they love us and want to honor us.

So does God.

And so we work for our Lord because our Lord is also our Dad who loves us deeply. He always has and He always will. We don't work to get to heaven, but because we're already going. We don't work to get God's love; we work because we've already got it.

Dear Abba,

I ask that you plant firmly in my heart the absolute assurance that I am saved. I am saved by your grace through faith in your Son Jesus, and I thank you for that incredible gift! Make me know without a doubt that I am delivered from death and reconciled to you. And make me completely unshakeable in that knowledge! Remove all the remnants of fear and anxiety that the enemy uses against me. Take away any lingering dread that I might not be doing enough to be saved.

I ask you to rekindle a spirit of diligence to move in my personal ministry of reconciling others to you. I ask you to position and empower me to do more and greater things for your glory.

And I pray that you always help me maintain a spiritually healthy sense of balance in how I see you. Never let me lose my reverence for you and my fear of your wrath against sin. But never let me lose sight of your love for sinners like me and your deep desire to be my loving Father. In the name of Jesus, amen!

8

―――――

Your Name Is On the Building

There were two young men who worked in middle management for a successful manufacturing company in a booming town. The first one rushed to get to work a half hour early every day, stressed and frazzled from the time he hit the door. Already on his second cup of coffee as he entered the factory, he worked tirelessly to please everyone, both his superiors and his subordinates.

He worked through most of his breaks, desperately trying to curry favor with everyone around him. He was always asking people to put in a good word for him with the higher-ups and seemed to live in constant fear that his first mistake at the company would be his last. He stayed late nearly every afternoon, burning himself out with more and more work, much of which wasn't even in his job description.

In contrast, the other young man arrived every day with calm confidence, never late, but never extra early either. He did his job well, didn't seem to sweat much of anything, and went home each day (on time) with a smile. He was firm, but fair, with those under him. He was respectful to those over him, but he never sucked up to them and never lobbied for position or promotion.

The more work the first guy did, the more his co-workers were happy to let him do, so the load kept getting heavier and heavier. One day it got to be too much to bear. After a particularly stressful meeting, he went outside and hid behind the building, trying to hold it together. He wanted to scream and cry and punch something all at once.

After several minutes of pacing and fuming and pep-talking himself off the proverbial ledge, he went back inside. There he saw the second young man, who had been in the same nerve-wracking meeting, calmly sitting in the break room, sipping coffee and thumbing through a magazine. He started to go back to work, but this time, he had to say something.

"How do you do it, man?" he asked.

"How do I do what?" his counterpart replied.

"How do you keep it together like you do? You never get stressed out! How are you sitting here like this after that meeting we just had? Working here is killing me, but every day seems like a day at the park for you! You gotta tell me, man. How do you do it?"

"Oh, that's easy," the second young man answered calmly. "My name is on the building."

He went back to reading his magazine and sipping his coffee. After a moment of contemplation, the first guy looked closely at his co-worker's name badge. Sure enough, his last name, which he had never noticed before, was the very same name on every sign, every shirt, and every piece of stationery around him. All this time, he had been working with the owner's son, and being a son made all the difference in the world.

Guess what? Your name is on the building!

Your Father owns the whole thing. That's why Paul could write in 1 Corinthians 3:21 to remind the believers, "All things are yours." You're God's child. YOU'RE GOD'S CHILD! This means that what's His is yours. As children of God, we're heirs of God. And we're heirs together with Jesus, so we stand to gain everything He received as a beloved Son of the Father (Romans 8:17).

Glory and honor are already yours! Victory and vindication are already yours! Peace and joy are already yours! You may not feel like you have all these things just yet, but they're your inheritance as God's child. All of this and more is reserved for you by the will and testament of Jesus Christ, and nothing can stop it from coming to you at the appointed time.

When your name is on the building, you don't need to compete with other people for stuff that's already yours! You don't have to be a devious, underhanded person, always looking to thwart someone else's progress so that you can advance. You don't feel the need to sabotage someone else's work or ruin the next person's reputation to get the things you want in life.

You know that your Father is infinitely wealthy and He has plenty to go around. And you know that what He has for you is just for you; no one else is going to get your blessing. Walking in your sonship means that you move through life with the peace of knowing that you're going to be taken care of, no matter what.

When your name is on the building, you don't need to prove yourself to people who ultimately hold no power over you! You don't feel compelled to compromise your values or act out of character in order to convince others to accept you, award you, or appreciate you. You don't need to act or speak or dress or live in a way that's not who you are to gain the fleeting favor of man. You don't have to suck up to anyone. You know that simply walking in righteousness and integrity will find favor in the eyes of your Father, and *that* favor will take you farther than the world's approval ever will.

You're the Owner's son, and being a son makes all the difference in the world.

Dear Abba,

Thank you for the peace of knowing that I'm your child. Let that knowledge release me from a life of frantic desperation and fretful anxiety. When I forget that my name is on the building, bring my heart back to that place of perfect peace in knowing that you take care of your own. Remind me that everything is yours—all the cattle in every pasture, all the fish in every sea, and every single star in the sky! And remind me to trust that, as your heir, what's yours is mine!

Thank you for your promise to provide. Help me to take you at your word and to walk with you in faith even when my situation makes it hard to believe. Take away the spirit of competition from me and keep me from ever feeling like I have to fight other people over your blessings. Take away from my heart the need to have the approval of other people and help me to focus on your favor as my all-powerful Father. Teach me to be joyfully at rest in my relationship with you, always remembering who I am and whose I am. In the precious name of Jesus, amen!

9

The Reason for the Season

Sonship even changes how you see your storms. Walking with God doesn't guarantee a perfectly pleasant existence. Remember, sometimes you'll be walking with Him through the valley of the shadow of death!

Many of life's seasons will be extremely difficult and excruciatingly painful. Believers who see God solely as Master and Lord often experience deep spiritual confusion, frustration, and pain during these times. This is because they wrongly believe that all of the hardships of life are the wrath of a disappointed and disapproving Judge being poured out upon them.

We feel that way as little children. Sometimes our kids will ask me and their mother why we're "being so mean" when we chastise them. I can remember feeling the same way about my parents at times. We all can. We thought they didn't want us to have any fun. We wondered if they got some perverse pleasure out of being so tough on us and making our lives harder than they had to be.

We couldn't understand why our parents wanted us to look like losers to our friends because we couldn't stay out late with them on a school night.

We couldn't grasp what the correlation between candy and cleaning up was, why we couldn't have one because we hadn't done the other.

We couldn't fathom why they were making us forfeit our allowance to pay for the damage instead of just taking care of it with their own money, of which they had plenty, by the way. After all, they just had to go out back and pick some off the money tree. What's the big deal?

But then we grew up. We came to realize over time that none of the spankings, groundings, lectures, or confiscations were intended to hurt us—they were actually meant to help us. While the wrath of God against sin is real, scripture encourages those of us who know Him as Father to view His discipline as corrective and constructive.

Hebrews 12 tells us to see our suffering as the discipline of a Father who loves us dearly and deeply. He's treating us like His own children because, well, we *are*! The writer asks rhetorically in verse 7, "What son is there whom his father does not discipline?" Fathers punish and chastise and correct their children. It's what they do. The good ones, anyway. And they do it because they love their children and want the best for them.

This is how you need to see the trying times that you go through as a believer. These times are not just random seasons of hardship. They're not bad breaks or terrible luck. And they're not the spiteful whims of a cruel and vindictive deity. These trying times are divinely-sanctioned situations. The motivation behind them is the love that Father God has for you as His child, and the intended outcome is your spiritual growth.

Walking in your sonship means living with the confidence that, whatever your Father is allowing to happen, He's permitting it for a purpose. And that purpose is to perfect you! If you ask a thousand parents why they do what they do for their children—from providing to punishing, from rewarding the good to reprimanding the bad—nearly all of the answers would boil down to some form of this one simple truth: we want them to become the best versions of themselves.

We see what our children could be, and we want them to realize that potential. We know what they're good at, and we want them to be moving in their giftedness. We recognize their weaknesses, and we want to help them grow and improve in those areas.

God sees His children the same way. And His perfect knowledge and divine insight far surpasses that of even the most attuned human parent. If we think we know our children, how much more does an all-knowing God know His?

So what it comes down to is trust.

When you're going through a season of sickness, can you trust that your Abba knows that this is exactly what you need to slow you down or to help you regain your perspective and reset your priorities?

When you're dealing with financial problems or family issues, can you trust that your Abba sees something in your character that needs fine-tuning or some deficiency in your heart that needs dealing with?

When you're going through a season of loss, can you trust that your Abba knows you need to be on this side of things for a while, that you need to develop empathy so you can minister more effectively to those who are hurting?

When you're dealing with the difficult consequences of your wrong choices and actions, can you trust that your Abba knows you need to be humbled, that you often need to be led—maybe even a bit firmly at times—to apologize or to make things right?

Can you trust that He sees some impurities that are imperceptible to you when you look in the mirror? Can you trust that there are some lessons you need to learn and some wisdom you need to gain for the next level of life?

When you really start to see God as your Father, you rest in the assurance that, for reasons you can't completely comprehend, this obstacle, this pain, this struggle is exactly what He knows you need to get where He knows you can go.

And so there's a stillness in your spirit even as your body agonizes or your finances fall apart. There's a Jesus-peace in the midst of the raging storm. There's a sense of submission to the Father's purpose and even a sense of gratitude for the problems He's using to bring that purpose about.

Even as you pray for the deliverance you *want*, you still trust Him to give you what you *need*. Of course you long for relief from your pain, but you also realize that the pain has a purpose that may not yet be fulfilled. And so you say to your trusted Father, just as the Son Himself said, "Not my will, but yours be done."

Dear Abba,

I thank you for loving me enough to correct me and perfect me. Thank you for the deeper understanding of my storms. I pray that you never allow them to cause me to doubt your love for me, but that you'll always give me the eyes to see them as loving discipline and careful guidance from you.

I pray for the faith to trust you when I'm struggling. Help me to trust that you know what's best for me, that you know exactly what I need to grow into who you want me to be. I pray for the wisdom, humility, and patience to learn the lessons that I need to learn from my trials. Give me the clarity to discern your purpose in whatever problems I may be going through.

I pray that my growing relationship with you will bring a greater and greater peace when I'm facing my seasons of hardship. I pray for the peace of Jesus Himself to be upon me and to protect me in every storm. In His blessed name, amen!

10

More Than a Title

Speaking of Abba, you need to understand that word. The Spirit is trying to tell you something vitally important about the fullness of your relationship with God. See, the Aramaic word "Abba" is what we call a vocative. It's a word that's used to address someone or to get someone's attention. In other words, it's not what a person *is*; it's what you *call* them when you're talking to them.

Think about it for a minute: how many people do you know who call their mother "Mother" when they speak to her? Have you ever heard a little girl scream, "Grandfather!" when her grandfather showed up passing out candy and coins? Did you ever once call your father "Father"? Probably not. I know I never did. You knew that's what he *was*, and you may have referred to him as your father when you were talking to someone else *about* him, but what you called him when you were talking *to* him was Dad or Daddy or Pops. You called your mother Mama or Mommy. You called your grandfather Gramps or Papa.

The truth is, on those rare occasions when we *do* hear someone call their father "Father" or call their mother "Mother," we raise an eyebrow. It just sounds weird. It makes us think something's off. It's stilted and stuffy. It makes us wonder if there's any affection in the relationship, or just fear. It seems like they're lacking a connection that families who live and laugh and cry and eat and fight and play together ought to have.

So God *is* your Father, but you can *call* Him "Abba." Abba isn't formal—it's familiar. It suggests closeness and intimacy. It's like Daddy or Papa. It's not a title; it's a term of endearment. It carries fondness and adoration.

Let that sink in. The great God of all that is, the awesome and all-powerful Master of the entire universe gives you and me permission to address Him with the same familiarity and affection as we do our parents and loved ones! That's amazing, and it should be wonderfully encouraging to you!

I've heard from people smarter than me that the word "Abba" would be used by older Jewish children, pre-teens and up, who loved their fathers, but who also were growing into some idea of who their fathers were to them and to the community. They were starting to have a sense of appreciation for who this man was, not just in the home, but also in the neighborhood and the marketplace. "Abba" carried love and respect and admiration from the lips of the child to the ears of the father.

If God hasn't yet become Abba to you, that may suggest something about the nature of your relationship. It's good that you know that He *is* your Father, but if all you ever *call* Him is "Father," then you may not have grown into the fullness of intimacy, affection, and trust that He wants you to enjoy with Him. And, yes, He *wants* you to enjoy this type of familiarity with Him.

Study Romans 8:15 and its context. Take note that it's the Spirit of God who puts into us the love and joy and knowledge to call Him Abba. It doesn't disrespect or dishonor God to speak to Him in familiar and intimate terms. How can it? He's the one who tells us to do it!

One of the wonderful paradoxes of the Christian life is that we have both reverence for God and intimacy with God. They're not mutually exclusive; we can do both. We can worship Him as Creator and King, but we also have His permission to call Him Papa. We can bow down before Him as the Almighty, and then we can climb into His lap and cozy up to Him as Abba. We say, "hallowed be thy name," right after we greet Him as "our Father."

Remember, the work of Jesus was restorative in nature. He came to reconcile us to God, something all the formality of religious observance and ritualistic worship could never do. He came to take us back to the beginning, back to when we were walking with Him in the garden. Back to when we were close to God, when we were *comfortable* with God. Back to a time when He was the only Daddy man had ever known.

Dear Abba,

I thank you today for permission to call you my Abba! I rejoice in the fact that you want to have a warm and personal relationship with me. Thank you for allowing me to be intimate with you.

You are awesome and holy and worthy of reverence, and I give you all the glory and honor that you deserve. I exalt you as God Most High and I bow down before you as Creator and King of the whole universe! But I'm so glad that you're not just a cold, impersonal God. I'm so glad that, as high and holy as you are, you haven't made yourself distant and unapproachable. Thank you for still welcoming your precious little children into your arms.

Teach me to walk in the warmth of a full and familiar relationship with you. May your Spirit continue to show me how much you want me to be close to you and comfortable with you, even while I hold you in reverence. Thank you for being my God and thank you for being my Dad. I pray in the beautiful name of Jesus, amen!

11

Use Your Outside Voice

Up to this point, I've been talking about how we can *call* God Abba, and that's true. By His Spirit in us, we're empowered and privileged to speak to God intimately and to cultivate a close personal relationship with Him. If you've ever heard someone teach on this passage, that's probably where they left it. I think that's sound and powerful teaching, but that's not all Romans 8:15 is saying to us.

Notice another very important word in that verse: the word "cry." Paul doesn't simply say that we *call* God Abba; he says that we *cry*, "Abba!"

The Greek word that's translated as "cry" in that verse was used to describe the screeching of a crow. It's alarming and shrill. It's a loud, piercing cry that would definitely get your attention. So Paul wasn't just saying that we can *talk* to God; he was saying that we can *cry out* to God. There's a difference. He's literally saying that we *scream*, "ABBA!"

Now, I don't know about you, but I don't go around screaming at people in normal conversations. Shouting is reserved for special circumstances. We only scream and shout when we're experiencing intense emotions.

Think about this for a minute. There were countless times as a kid when you addressed your parent calmly and conversationally as Mommy or Daddy.

"Mommy, I need money for lunch."

"Dad, can I borrow the car?"

"Mom, did you wash my uniform?"

"I love you, Daddy."

From my own kids, I always hear, "Daddy, can I have a piece of candy?" They seem to always ask me instead of their mother for some reason. I don't know why, but I'm sure it has nothing to do with how much candy I let them have. That can't be it. (Don't judge me.) Anyway, the point is, I hear my "name" from their lips all the time in everyday life, and sometimes I even ignore what they're saying when it doesn't sound all that urgent. (Don't judge me, I said.)

But then there are times when I can't ignore it. Those are the times when they're not *saying*, "Daddy," but they're *screaming*, "DADDY!"

One night I was awakened by my son shouting to me from the top of the stairs. He was in a sweaty panic and he was screaming in terror. He was having a fever dream, and whatever he had seen had him scared. So what was the first thing he did? He screamed, "DADDY!" And the first thing I did when I heard him? I jumped up and took off running!

When they scream, "Mommy!" or "Daddy!" we know something's wrong. The tone and volume of our children's voices lets us know this isn't a normal circumstance or an ordinary request. They don't *want* us—they *need* us.

Sometimes they're screaming out of fear; there's a nightmare or a dog or a spider. Sometimes they're screaming out of pain because they've skinned a knee or broken an arm. Sometimes they're screaming out of sadness—maybe they've heard some distressing news or broken a favorite toy. Whatever the emotion behind it, they know instinctively to cry out to the people who have loved them and comforted them and cared for them all along.

Part of walking in your sonship means learning to stop praying pretty prayers. Many of us learned to pray very formally, even formulaically. A lot of us got the mistaken belief in us along the way that when you talk to God, you have to compose yourself before you speak and make it very neat and tidy and respectful. Despite the enormity of the emotions you're feeling, you'd better button it down before you bring it to the Lord or you run the risk of offending or disrespecting Him somehow.

Get over that!

Paul says that God's Spirit within us will have us screaming, "Abba!" Again, when do we scream? We scream when we're terrified. We scream when we're ecstatic. We scream when we're hurting. We scream when we're angry. Not when we're cool, calm, and collected.

Consider the Son Himself. As Jesus was nearing the cross, Mark 14:34–36 tells us that His soul was so heavy with pain, He felt like He was about to die. He was terrified. He was in emotional agony. He was on the ground trembling with His face in the dirt. His sweat was running down like drops of blood. That's when the Son cried, "Abba!" That's when His spirit screamed for Daddy, begging to be released from the awful assignment He had been given.

So in Romans 8, Paul is writing about how we talk to God in times of intense suffering and extreme emotion. He's telling us that God doesn't expect us to suppress our feelings and address Him formally with religious rhetoric and eloquent supplications when our world is crumbling around us.

What He expects, what He wants from His children is such a strong and trusting relationship with their Abba that they just instinctively cry out to Him for the help they need. That they unabashedly release to Him all of their emotions, positive and negative. That they can be so raw and so reliant on Him that they hold *nothing* back.

Here's the thing—when my kids scream for me, I love it! Well, not right away. Initially, I'm scared and panicked because I don't know what's happening. Or sometimes I'm frustrated and annoyed when I hear them shouting for me. (I kept telling them to stop playing so rough, and now, of course, somebody's hurt!) So, no, I don't love it right away.

But after I calm down and pass out the ice-packs or get them back to sleep, after the fear or the frustration subsides and I find a silent moment, I love the fact that they cried out for me! I'm glad that they didn't hesitate in their moment of personal crisis to shout for me or their mother. I feel happy and blessed that our relationship is such that they don't even think about what to do or who to call.

There's no fear or embarrassment or shame. They just do exactly what they're supposed to do in that moment—they scream for Daddy.

Dear Abba,1

I'm so glad that I can come to you with all of my pain, all of my fear, all of my sorrow. Thank you for the grace of your sympathy and understanding. It comforts me to know that I don't have to hold back or hold it in when I'm going through a storm. It comforts me to know that I can call out to you in any state of mind, knowing that you want to hear from me as your child.

I praise you for your loving and attentive heart! I praise you as the compassionate Father you are, a Father whose ears are open to His precious children, just like our ears are open to our own. Help me to hold onto the assurance that I don't have to be ashamed to cry out to you, that I don't have to dress it up or tone it down when I'm hurting.

I pray for a heart that instinctively calls out to you as my first priority, not as my last resort. I pray for a spirit of total trust in you, a spirit of absolute confidence in your desire to hear my voice. In the wonderful name of Jesus, amen!

12

Teach Us To (Really) Pray

Sometimes my kids even scream *at* Daddy. My son is good for that. When he gets frustrated or angry with me, there's this certain way he says my "name." It sounds like this: "DAAADDDDYYYYY!!!" His anger is written all over his face, and he just lets loose. Sometimes I have to warn him not to cross the line, but I don't mind him venting his frustrations. I want him to tell me what he thinks I did wrong. I want to hear about why he's mad and try to understand it. I want to understand *him*.

Plus, I'm a grown man, so I can take the anger of a six-year-old. I try not to laugh, but it's even a little funny sometimes. It's serious to him, of course, but from my adult perspective, what he's mad about is usually pretty small in the grand scheme of things. I'm sure part of him wants to hit me. He hasn't yet, but even if he did, it wouldn't do much damage.

My son's anger isn't a real threat to me, and I don't take it as one because I'm his father and I know he loves me. And I know that he knows I love him. He's just hot right now, but he'll eventually cool off. He just needs to vent. He just needs an explanation. Or a hug. Or all of the above. And then we're good again, usually pretty quickly.

Get this in your spirit: neat and tidy and respectful isn't what God wants from our conversation with Him, especially in the difficult seasons of life.

There are some very messy prayers in scripture. Some even sound pretty disrespectful! But these prayers were lifted by real people going through real storms who had a real relationship with God. The relationship was real and strong enough that they felt free to give Him their whole hearts, even the parts we try to gloss over and hide when we're in polite company.

The frustration.

The disappointment.

The rage.

Jeremiah's a great example. Read chapter 20 of his book. He had been beaten and put in the stocks for speaking God's word. He was sore physically and emotionally from being mistreated for doing the very thing God called him to do. He felt like he had been played. He felt like this wasn't what he had signed up for. And so his spirit screamed, "Daddy, I'm mad at you!"

Get this—Jeremiah actually accused God of tricking him and taking advantage of him! It wasn't *factual*, but it was how Jeremiah was *feeling*. And God permitted him to pour it all out.

One of the blessings of real, raw prayer is that the sooner you get your feelings out of the way, the sooner you can get back to the facts. The sooner you can come back to a place of spiritual peace and stability. When you read that chapter, notice how quickly Jeremiah went from "Lord, you deceived me" to "Praise the Lord!" The prophet gave it all over to God, and in no time his spirit had settled back into a posture of trust and submission.

Once his eyes were no longer clouded with anger, Jeremiah could see clearly again. He could see that the Lord was with Him. He could see that his God was greater than any foe who came against him. He could see that everything was going to be alright, even when it wasn't.

My eyes got big the first time I read Jeremiah's prayer. I could hardly believe what I was reading. You can't talk to God like that...can you? Well, apparently you can! Jeremiah survived. God didn't strike him down or make the ground open up and swallow him whole.

But we struggle with that because that's not how we're taught to pray. At least not by religious people. The Holy Spirit certainly does teach us to pray that way because it's in the scriptures. The problem is that we often pay more attention to our *religious* teachers than we do to our *spiritual* Teacher.

Jeremiah 20 has been in the Bible all along, and when we embrace the prophet's example, we'll start praying some radically real, surprising, even seemingly offensive prayers. And these prayers actually please God more than all the fake, fancy fluff we learned in Sunday school!

God can take it. He's omnipotent, and He knows it. He's not threatened or intimidated by my angry outbursts any more than I am by my six-year-old's. He's not going to strike me down because He feels the need to assert Himself and remind me who I'm talking to. He's patient and He's compassionate.

The Father smiles to Himself while His children vent. He graciously lets us get it all out. He knows we love Him, and He knows that we know He loves us. So we unleash our fury and we wear ourselves out. Then He gives us a hug and a glass of water, and everything's good again.

Consider His compassion for a moment. Our Father knows what we need and He wants to help us. He knows that our emotions are natural and necessary. But He also knows that when those feelings aren't given voice, they tend to turn into something else.

Unspoken frustration becomes resentment.

Unspoken hurt becomes bitterness.

Unspoken anger becomes rage.

Unspoken fear becomes despair.

And what the feeling turns into as it festers is always worse than what it was at first. So Abba lets us talk to Him. He mercifully and patiently lets us purge those feelings before they become something dangerous and destructive.

If you struggle praying like this, consider another truth: your Father already knows how you're feeling anyway. Just like we already have a pretty good sense of what our own kids are going through before they even say a word. We live with them long enough and we learn what makes them tick. Eventually, we can read them like we read a book. We know precisely what *that* face means when they make it. We know exactly how they're feeling when we hear that certain vocal inflection.

So if we can read our kids, you better believe that the all-knowing, all-seeing, everywhere-all-at-once God that we call Abba can definitely read His! God has always known His children. He knew us before we were even formed in the womb. He doesn't just hear words and interpret tone and read body language—He searches hearts. Whatever you're *really* going through, He already knows.

So what really honors and pleases Him is when we show enough trust to be honest with Him and just tell Him what He already knows. It honors Him and it helps us. I believe that God is far more pleased with an angry, frustrated prayer that tells Him the unfiltered truth about what you're going through than He is with any stoic, formal petition that suppresses real emotion and simply says all the things we think we're supposed to say to God.

He can take it. The truth is, He *wants* it. And the deeper truth is, He wants *you.*

The greatest commandment we have from God is to love Him with *all* of our hearts. Your anger is a part of your heart. So is your frustration and your fear and your confusion. And He's the one who gave you that heart with the capacity to feel all this stuff in the first place.

So start praying your *heart.* Not a script. Not an impersonal form letter. Not what someone else has told you to say to God. Start praying your heart. However calm or turbulent, however ecstatic or despondent. Even if it's broken. Your Father gave it to you. Now He wants you to give it to Him.

Being a child of Abba God means you don't have to hold anything back.

Dear Abba,

I thank you so much for the patience you have with your people. Thank you for your understanding of our emotions and for the grace you give us to release them to you. You know who we are and you know what we feel. Thank you for allowing me to vent even my deepest frustrations and my hottest anger to you. You're a big enough God that you can take it all, and you're a gracious enough God to let me purge my spirit of the things that can weigh me down.

Teach me to give you my whole heart. Teach me to have enough trust in your love for me that I can give you everything that's inside of me. I pray for my relationship with you to deepen and grow, to become more real and open and sincere.

Thank you for being there to take all my feelings and exchange them for a faith that's more firm than ever before. In Jesus' name, amen!

13

From Your Lips To His Ear

My son is a quiet talker. Sure, like any kid, he's wild and loud at home. (As I'm writing this, I'm wishing that he and his sister would take it down a few notches!) But when we're around other people, it's a totally different story. He practically whispers when we're in public.

He's painfully shy. I was the same kid, so I guess the acorn doesn't fall far from the tree. Anyway, we're always asking him to repeat himself and speak up. So he supposedly raises his voice and says it again, like a tenth of a decibel louder. And we still can't hear him.

Sometimes the only way for me to hear what my son is saying—especially when we're someplace crowded and noisy—is to bend down and put my ear right next to his mouth.

Psalm 40:1 paints a brief, but beautiful, picture of Dad Most High. David says, "He inclined to me and heard my cry." In his time of weakness, in his pain and desperation, David lifted his little voice up to God. And God, who was in no way obligated to respond...God, who is infinitely higher and holier than wretched creatures like us...God, who has a whole universe of things to be concerned about, bent down and put His ear right to His son's lips! You need to know that you have a caring, compassionate Father who leans in and listens.

When you're so exhausted that you can barely muster the strength to form the words.

When you're so confused that you can't even think straight, let alone put your thoughts into coherent sentences.

When you're choking on your tears and you're gasping for your breath.

When everyone else you were counting on is too distracted to listen or just downright doesn't want to be bothered.

When the clamor of all the chaos swirling around you seems to be drowning out every attempt to get a clear message through, your gracious God bends over and leans in close so He can hear what's on the heart of His child.

At times in my life, I've been ashamed to pray. I knew I needed to, but I didn't want to. I knew I *could* and I *should*, but I didn't feel worthy. So in my guilt and shame, I "whispered" to God. I didn't come boldly to the throne like Jesus empowers me to do. I came timidly and awkwardly. I came with my head hung low, bashfully speaking under my breath. But despite the near-silence of my sheepish plea, He heard me anyway.

Because He leaned in and He listened.

Some of the places He has to lean in to listen to us are places that an awesome and holy God has no business being. But He leans in anyway. David said in the very next verse that he was in a deep pit of murky clay. *That's* where the Lord had to lean over and lift His son out of. To His glory, the Father is never afraid to get some dirt on Him in order to get His children out of trouble!

When our kids get themselves into a pit, as parents, we still go pull them out. It costs us time and energy. We have to miss work and burn money we were hoping to spend on other things. It takes us to some places we never thought we'd go. But we're right there with them in the courthouse or the hospital or the jail or wherever. Even when they put themselves in that predicament, we're still right there with them.

That's a parent's love, and our heavenly Father's love for His children is no less than our love for our own. In fact, His is even greater than ours! His is perfect and pure and unsearchably deep. His is thoroughly unconditional and completely untainted by any human brokenness.

One of the great comforts of your life as a believer should be in knowing you have a Father who hears you. He hears you on your sick bed. He hears you from your prison cell. He hears you from your closet of loneliness. Don't *ever* think that He doesn't. Wherever you are, whatever you're going through, whatever you're saying, His ear is right next to your lips.

One of my favorite lines ever comes from the song "Just a Little Talk with Jesus." The line goes, "He'll hear our faintest cry, and answer by and by." If you've been a parent of babies or toddlers, you get it. You know that whatever else is going on, you can *always* hear your children when they cry out. It's almost miraculous! It's like this weird sixth sense that only a parent has.

And each parent's antenna is tuned specifically to their own child! Everyone can hear it when your kid is screaming at the top of their lungs, but somehow only *you* can hear their "faintest cry."

The television can be on and the kid can be on a completely different level of the house with a couple of closed doors between you, but somehow you hear that fragile little voice whimpering in the dark. Even if you're asleep, something about that tiny voice still kicks you right out of your slumber and puts you on the alert! (Except for my wife. Somehow I'm the only one who ever wakes up for our kids. Other than that, she's a *fantastic* mother. Really.)

Your Abba's wired the same way. (Where do you think we get it from?) There's nothing that can interfere with the sound of His children's voices. There's never too much going on. There's never too much noise. It doesn't matter what's trying to come between you and keep you apart. It doesn't matter how softly you speak. The Father *always* hears His children.

And He answers by and by.

Dear Abba,

Thank you for loving me enough to lean in and listen to my little voice! I'm so glad and so grateful that, as big as you are, you're not too big to hear my smallest cares and my faintest cries. I don't always know what to say or how to say it, but I know that you hear me just the same, and that brings me so much peace.

Thank you for coming to get me when I had put myself in some bad places. Your mercy is so wonderful! You didn't have to bail me out, but you did. You didn't have to give me another chance, but you did. You didn't have to save me, but you did.

When the world makes me feel insignificant, help me to overcome those feelings of unworthiness. When the enemy stirs up my insecurities, help me to hold on to your love for me. Never let me forget that I'm the most important thing in the world to you. Remind me that wherever I am and whatever I need, you hear me. And help me to trust that your answer is on the way. In Jesus' name, amen!

14

Kids Will Be Kids

I love what David wrote in Psalm 103:13. In another of his many beautiful songs, he penned the line, "As a father shows compassion to his children, so the LORD shows compassion to those who fear Him."

And the reason? Verse 14 says it's because He knows how we were formed—He remembers that we're only dust. We were formed from it and we're going back to it. We're frail and we're finite. God takes pity on us because He knows we're pitiful.

I'm glad God isn't like us. Sometimes I forget that my children are just children. I forget that they don't know everything I know. That they're not as big or strong or fast as I am. That they don't have the life experience and the frame of reference for certain things that I have. And when I forget what they are, I push them too hard. I get frustrated with them, then my frustration starts to frustrate them. And it's not good for our relationship.

When my son was first learning to play the piano—he was five at the time—I pushed a little too hard. I knew what I was doing, and I thought his little song was pretty easy. I had been there and done that. But I forgot that he was just starting. That this was all new to him and he was still unsure of himself. I forgot that his little hands were only half the size of mine. So after a testy exchange between us, he groaned out loud, got up from the keyboard, and stormed off!

My first emotion was indignation. I was angry that he wasn't getting it, and now I was even angrier that he had the nerve to walk away from me. How dare he! But after a second—and before I could react, thankfully—I realized that little debacle was on me. That wasn't the son failing to do something he was capable of doing; that was the father failing to see clearly what the son could and couldn't do.

That was me not remembering that he was just a kid.

Our Father never forgets! He never forgets that His children are just children. That we're feeble, flawed little things. That there's a lot we don't know. His thoughts about us never lapse into the realm of unrealistic expectation. His perception is perfect; He always sees us for exactly what we are. Abba knows what we can do and He knows what we can't do, even when we don't know ourselves!

When it comes to His little children, God is gentle and merciful. He's tenderhearted and sympathetic toward us. He knows our limitations, and He's longsuffering with us. What a powerful truth!

Our Father is not harsh and demanding. He's not callous and coldhearted. He isn't indifferent to our struggles. We often think of God in those ways because of our mischaracterization of Him or our mistaken assumptions about Him. Sometimes we even take our negative and hurtful experiences with our not-so-great human parents and transfer them to our heavenly Parent. But the scripture clearly tells us that's not Him at all. When you know the truth, the truth will set you free from the bondage of broken thinking about God.

The truth is, your Abba knows that you're all-too-human and that your human heart gets wounded, your human mind gets misdirected, and your human body gets exhausted.

Your Abba knows that you've got some junk in you from your past experiences, some baggage that you're still carrying around, some brokenness that gets in the way of you being your best self.

Your Abba knows the addictive effects of sin on the human heart and that your carnal desires didn't just dissipate completely the second you were saved.

Your Abba knows that you're still learning and growing and trying, that you're not on His level and you never will be.

He knows all of this, and He treats you accordingly. He treats you with patience. He's slow to anger. He continues to lovingly lead you through your mistakes and your missteps, tenderly but firmly guiding your growth. Just like we do for our children.

Now, don't get this twisted. There's a difference between a sin of weakness and a sin of willfulness. One sneaks up on you; the other, you run headlong into its arms. One, God deals with patiently; the other, He deals with punitively.

Paul warned in Romans 6:1–2 against treating God's grace like it's a license to live unrighteously. Be grateful that He's gracious, but don't ever start to take His mercy and forgiveness for granted. Remember, Psalm 103:13 says that the Father's compassion is for those who *fear* Him, not for those who flout His will.

And let me say this while we're on the subject: no matter how old you are, you're still God's *child*. You may have grown up and long since moved out of your parents' house. You may have had a lengthy career and made lots of your own money. You may have titles to your name and authority over a whole lot of people. Your hair may be gray or it may be gone altogether. You're still God's child.

You're small and weak and ignorant compared to His bigness, His strength, and His wisdom. You still need your Dad, and you always will. It's important that you understand yourself that way in relation to Him, that you never stop seeing yourself in that light. It's important that you stay in your place.

God hates pride in us because it shows that we've lost perspective on who we really are and who He really is. Pride drives us farther from Him. Like the rebellious child who wrestles his hand away from his mom or dad's caring grip so he can go after what he wants, pride makes us foolishly pull away from our Protector and our Provider. Always to our own detriment, sometimes even to our own demise.

But back to that powerful truth David shared. When you know that your Father sees you with compassionate eyes, you begin to trust in His goodness toward you. You don't fear that He's going to drop the hammer every time you make a mistake. You're relieved to know that He doesn't look with contempt on your weakness or grow to despise you just because you struggle to do something. You take comfort from the fact that He's always careful not to put more on you than you can handle.

I had to apologize to my son after I pushed him too hard. I had to admit that I was expecting too much and not giving him the space and time he needed to grow. That allowed us to reconnect. And when we tried to practice again, he began to thrive under the patient guidance I started to give. The frustration was gone, replaced by a calmness and that grew into confidence on his part. He was relaxed and comfortable under my tutelage once he sensed that I was seeing him for what he was and treating him accordingly.

Moving in relationship with your Abba means being at peace in His presence, the peace of knowing that He knows you and trusting that He's setting just the right pace for your progress. It's being comfortable under the firm, yet gentle, guidance of His hand. It's resting easy in the assurance that the Father knows we're just kids.

And He knows that kids will be kids.

Dear Abba,

I praise you for your compassionate eyes and for your merciful heart! I thank you for knowing me completely as your child, for seeing my strengths and weaknesses, and for not holding my weaknesses against me. I'm grateful that you never forget who we are as human beings, that you never lose sight of the frailty of our fleshly nature.

I pray that I can always find peace in your awareness of my imperfections, while always seeking to be perfected. Let me never take your patience for granted; give me a heart that hungers for righteousness and diligently seeks after holiness. But let me always find comfort in knowing that, even when I fall short of your glory, you still love and accept me.

I pray for deeper trust in your absolute knowledge of who I am. Help me to trust that you see me through and through, that you know what I can and can't do. Never let me forget that you don't ever push your children too hard or put more on us than we can bear. In Jesus' glorious name, amen!

15

Daddy Doesn't Need the Money

Around the time I was in college and starting to work a few different jobs, my dad began making me and my brother pay "rent." I didn't go away for college and I didn't have much interest in moving out. I was content to stay home and save up my money so I could start married life right. And my parents were okay with me staying.

But at a certain point, I think they realized they'd be doing us a disservice if they just let two grown men stay in their house for free. So one day, my dad sat us down and let us know that if we wanted to stay, we'd have to kick in. Nothing major, just a hundred or so each month, depending on what we were getting paid.

By that point in my life, I had no problem doing it. Like I said before, I had come to realize how good I had it, so I was glad to be a blessing to my parents. I faithfully scratched a check to my father each month. Some months he even told me not to worry about it, maybe when my birthday rolled around or when Christmas was coming up. But I was consistent in making my "payments" and never gave the money a second thought.

Then it came time to move out. I had found my wife, and it was time to "leave and cleave," as they say. I had already stacked a good amount of money, so we were able to move right into our first house. As I said, I hadn't thought anymore about the money I had given my dad. As far as I was concerned, it was gone, spent on whatever he had deemed necessary for the household.

But one day, as I was preparing to move out, my father surprised me. He handed me a check for nearly the full amount of "rent" that I had paid him over the past few years! I don't remember exactly how much it was—a few thousand, I guess. But he gave it right back to me like it was nothing. And on top of that, he even paid for our honeymoon!

See, my dad didn't need the money; he just needed to know that I was willing to give it to him.

I want you to start thinking of your heavenly Father in that same way. Much is made in modern Christianity of our tithes and offerings. We're guilted into giving, shamed into giving, coerced into giving, and manipulated into giving. We're even flat-out lied into giving. That's why a lot of people avoid the church like the plague.

God just wants to *love* us into giving.

Walking in your sonship means being so thankful for your Abba's constant love and care that giving back to Him is nothing. There's no reluctance, no hesitation, no second thought. He deserves everything we could ever give Him and much, much more. And not just our money, but our time and our talents. Even our very selves.

And remember, Daddy doesn't need the money. Psalm 50:10–12 reminds us that He owns the cattle on a thousand hills! If He were hungry, He wouldn't bother to ask us for a snack. Everything is His—we're just enjoying it by His grace.

Understand that giving to your church or to a charity isn't doing God any good, at least not directly. You can't serve God *directly* because you don't have anything He needs. You can only serve Him *indirectly* by caring for those He cares about and loving those He loves. We can only serve God by serving each other. Jesus told us that whenever we feed a hungry person or visit a sick person or go see about someone in prison, we're doing it to Him. That's what He "needs." Daddy doesn't need the money...

He just needs to know that you're willing to give it to Him. He wants to know that you trust Him to do more with what you're giving away than you could ever do by keeping it. He wants to know that you know He can put it to good use. And He wants to know that you believe He's a multiplying God, that He can give it all back to you, and then some, whenever He gets ready!

When He knows you're willing—that you trust Him with everything you have—then He takes great pleasure in pouring out His abundance on you.

I'm sure my dad delighted in being able to give me that money back to help me start my new life, a life he had been preparing me for all along. Having children of my own now,

I can imagine his joy at the chance to do that! I believe Abba God revels in the opportunity to honor His children who honor Him.

Paul wrote in 2 Corinthians 9:7 that God loves a cheerful giver. He's reminding us that the Father's favor rests on those who show child-like faith in Him. The word "cheerful" comes from the same Greek word we get "hilarious" from. God delights in giving to those who delight in giving to Him.

I believe the happier you are to give to your Father, the happier your Father is to give back to you. For one thing, He knows He can trust you to do right with the abundance He's pouring into your life. He knows that the more good He gives you, the more good you'll do. Knowing that about His son or daughter makes Him proud.

And what's more, children of God who give freely look a whole lot like their Father! Giving is what God does. It's who He is. He gives and gives and keeps on giving. So He loves it when He sees the family resemblance in His kids!

Sometimes I just want to give my son something for no other reason than the fact that he looks like me, and that makes me feel good. When I look at my daughter's pretty little face and see myself, it makes me want to do something good for her. The likeness reminds me that they're mine and it makes me want to care for them all the more.

You better believe that when your Father sees Himself in you, His heart rejoices, His countenance smiles, and His hand moves to bless you in a big way!

Dear Abba,

Thank you for all the good things you've poured out on me, things I could never begin to number or name. I confess that I take so much for granted, and I ask your forgiveness for the times when I've failed to acknowledge you as the Giver of every good and perfect gift. You've been so good to me in so many ways!

Give me fresh eyes to see all the different ways you show me your mercy and grace. Give me a renewed spirit of thankfulness and a deeper appreciation of your love for me. And I pray that your love for me will reignite my love for you. Create a more generous heart in me, a heart that revels in the opportunities to honor you by helping others. Let me never become proud or entitled because of what I give, but help me to remember that it's just my reasonable service.

Renew my trust in you as a rewarding Master and a multiplying God. Remind me that I have nothing to lose by giving, but that I only stand to gain my Father's favor. In the holy name of Jesus I pray, amen!

16

Universe's Best Dad

I like to think I'm a pretty good dad. In fact, I have it on good authority from a very reliable coffee mug that I'm the world's *best* dad. Now, part of my greatness is my humility, so let's just say that I'm *one* of the world's best dads. But as great as I am, I'm still not a perfect father.

There are some days when I'm just too tired to care all that much, so I just say yes to everything and let my kids do whatever they want. Every now and then, I blow up and yell. It's very rare, but it happens. Some days I'm just too lazy to demand their best or to set a great example or to make them apologize to each other like I should.

So I'm a pretty good dad…most of the time. But despite all of my failures and weaknesses as a parent, there never has been and there never will be a time in my life when my kids ask me for something good and I intentionally give them something bad. I would never be so cruel as to give my hungry son a stone instead of bread or a snake instead of a fish. I'd never slip a poisonous spider into my daughter's lunchbox in place of her peanut butter and jelly sandwich!

Jesus says in Luke 11:11–13 that even the worst of us know how to be good to our kids. And if we, being imperfect, know how to do that, how much more does a perfect God know how to give good things to His children? We've got nothing on Him! So if *we* have a natural desire to bless our kids and see them happy, how much more does *He* want to shower His children with goodness and love?

And that doesn't always equate to material blessings either. In fact, most times it doesn't. Much of our modern "preaching" has made God out to be a glorified ATM, but He wants to give us so much more than money. The Father wants the *best* for His children, and that's the stuff you can't buy in a store. Wisdom. Peace. Guidance. Joy. Comfort. Love. Hope. All those fruits of the Spirit that make life worth living, much more than any material things ever could. Look at verse 13 again. That's actually what Jesus says the Father will give to those who ask— His Holy Spirit and all of the priceless, amazing gifts that come from His presence in our lives.

If you're a parent, think for a minute about all the things you've given your kids that they didn't exactly merit. If you're not a parent, think about everything your mom or dad or that good caregiver gave you that you didn't deserve. You may have never thought about it like this before, but if you start to tally it up, I guarantee that it's a *huge* list!

Think about all the birthday gifts and Christmas presents. All the trips to their favorite fast-food spots. All the random little toys and treats they talked you into getting for them on those everyday trips to the store. Think about all the movies you've taken them to see and all the play dates and sleepovers you've driven them to. All the clothes or shoes you bought them on a whim, not because they needed them, but just because they'd look so cute in them.

Think about all the things we do for our children that they don't earn, the countless little blessings that are in no way connected to them being good. Sure, we give them some things for getting a good report card or behaving extra well. But the vast majority of stuff we give our kids and do for our kids is in no way dependent on their performance.

In fact, a lot of that stuff is given in *spite* of their poor performance! They're not always well-behaved and they don't always do everything they're supposed to, but we do for them anyway. We do it because we love them and we love to see them happy.

You need to see your heavenly Abba's blessings—and His *willingness* to bless you—in the same way. He gives us so much, and He gives it so generously to imperfect children who really don't deserve any of it. And He loves doing it! Psalm 35:27 reminds us that the Lord takes great pleasure in blessing His people.

Of course, He doesn't give us *everything* we want, any more than we indulge every desire of our own children. But He gives us so much, and He wants to give us so much more. He wants us to come to *expect* good things from Him and to *ask* for them too.

God wants you to depend on Him as Daddy! He wants you to call on Him, knowing that He's listening, and to ask, knowing that an answer is on the way. He wants you to seek Him and pray for His blessings, trusting wholeheartedly that

He'll give what's good for you. He wants His children to knock on His door with total confidence and absolutely zero doubt that He's going to open up and let them in.

It's really too bad that so many of us actually expect scorpions and snakes. A lot of us have been taught by our bad experiences not to look for too much good out of life. Some people have been told so often and so emphatically that they're bad and worthless and undeserving that they've believed those lies and simply resigned themselves to the abuse and the hurt and the disappointment they think they deserve.

And many of us have been conditioned by religion to think that we've got to earn anything good that we get from God, that His blessings are all based on merit. So when we think about how good we *haven't* been and how little we've done for Him, we can't help but to feel like there's no way we really deserve a whole lot from Him in return.

The reality is that we often get what we expect to get. Do you know anyone who never expects things to go right? Someone who seems to go through life looking for disappointment and assuming things will fail? That person who's always preparing to be let down? It seems like, more often than not, they get what they're looking for.

Those people seem to manifest the very disappointments and defeats they keep talking about. Another relationship unravels—just like they thought it eventually would. They get sick again—just like they figured had to happen sooner or later. They lose another job—just like they predicted would inevitably occur.

Walking in your sonship means anticipating good things from a good Father. It means living with the peace and joy of knowing that He *wants* to bless you and that He *loves* to bless you. It means believing that, even though you don't always deserve them, good things are coming your way through your Abba's grace. So you ask for them boldly because He says you can! And your life of grateful obedience makes Him able to bless you all the more.

Dear Abba,

I praise you for your absolute goodness! You are good through and through. You are nothing but good, and you're good all the time! Thank you for the many ways you've shown that goodness in my life. Your patience. Your mercy. Your protection. Everything you've given me by your grace.

Thank you for giving me so much that I don't deserve, so much that I could never earn. Thank you that *your* goodness isn't dependent on *my* goodness! Teach me to walk in expectation of that goodness. Help me remember that you want to bless your children. Grow my confidence in your compassion for me. Take away from me the spirit of doubt and shame and self-pity and anything else that keeps me from walking in faith and hope.

And I pray for the conviction to move in obedience to your will for me as your child so that I can reap the fullness of this wonderful relationship I have with you through your Son. In His name, amen!

17

Welcome Home

You *have* to see how much your Father loves you. Granted, you'll never fully comprehend it. Not ever. But start meditating on it more often. Start spending more of your devotional time simply savoring God's love for you.

One verse of scripture I really love is 1 John 3:1. It's just a joyful exclamation of amazement over how much God loves us. John writes, "See what kind of love the Father has given to us, that we should be called children of God!"

When you stop and think about the incredible honor that a holy and awesome God bestows on broken, rebellious people like us—to be counted and treated as His very own offspring— it should really blow your mind! This love is astonishing. It's truly beyond belief.

One of the greatest depictions of this astounding love is found in Luke 15. That's where we read the story of the prodigal son. There's a lot to learn about ourselves from both the young man and his older brother, but there's also a lot to learn about how God sees His children and how deeply He cherishes them.

You probably know the story, so we don't have to start from the beginning. Let's start from the father's reaction to his wayward son's return. The story says that, one day, the father sees his son, but I also like to imagine that he *sees* his son because he was *looking* for his son. He never stopped thinking about him. He never put his boy out of his mind. He never moved on.

Every morning when the father goes outside to sweep the porch, he turns his eyes toward the road in hopes of seeing his long-lost son. Every night before he turns in, he looks out the window one more time, just in case. Then one glorious day, the father sees what he's been looking for—a lone silhouette on the horizon. Instantly, he knows the wait is over!

According to the story, the father sees his boy from a great distance. Now, imagine what he sees. Not only is he still far away, but add to that the fact that this person can't possibly look anything like the one who left. This one is wearing filthy, tattered rags, not an expensive, beautiful robe. His hair is a shaggy, matted mess, and his beard is overgrown and tangled. He's lost so much weight that he's literally half the man he used to be. He's not walking straight and tall anymore. He's hunched over and slowly dragging himself along, spending the last of his strength to reach his destination. His skin is caked with dirt, and his face is streaked with tears. This person is completely unrecognizable as the man who left home.

That is, to everyone except his father!

The father *knows* it's his son, and he knows right away. No amount of mud can disguise him. Somehow the father just knows that's his boy. From a mile away, he just knows! There's something in his gait that even the burden of the far country can't obscure. Or maybe there's something unmistakably familiar about the way he lifts his hand to shield his eyes from the sun. Whatever it is, this father knows his son when he sees him!

And then he runs to meet him. He doesn't turn away and pretend not to see him. He doesn't wait on the porch with his arms folded and force his son to complete every single step of his walk of shame. He doesn't give him the "Well, look who decided to come home" speech. No, he drops everything and takes off running at top-speed!

The words in the original language of the scripture mean that the father fell upon him and seized him. The man practically tackles his son when he reaches him! His unbridled elation takes them both to the ground. He grips his son tightly, weeping tears of joy as he clutches his boy's neck.

Now, think about who the father is embracing...

A disrespectful son who had impatiently demanded what was "his" and basically told his father he was taking too long to die!

A selfish boy who had turned his back on his family and run off to God-knows-where to do his own thing with no thought for what his parents must have been going through!

A wasteful, lascivious wretch who had defiled himself with prostitutes and blown his father's hard-earned wealth on the worst kinds of wickedness!

A broken, dirty young man who stinks of pigs, one who was not only socially humiliated, but spiritually sullied in the worst way!

That's who the father runs to embrace.

And he doesn't just hug him—he kisses him too. The original Greek is significant here, as well. It's not just one kiss. It's not just a quick peck on the cheek. The word means to kiss over and over again. The father literally showers his son with kisses! Before the boy had changed his clothes. Before he had even washed up. The father doesn't care what he looks like or what he smells like. His boy is alive, and he still loves him as much as he ever has.

Then he throws a party for his son, a full-blown, spare-no-expense celebration to mark this wonderful occasion. The father welcomes his boy back wholeheartedly and he makes sure that everyone in the house knows where his son stands— he's still his son! Despite the boy's humble plea to simply be received as a servant. Despite how he's defiled himself and disrespected his family. Despite all the time that's passed, the father still sees him as nothing less than a son.

The father puts sandals on his son's feet—a clear separation from the servants, who typically went barefoot. He puts a robe on his back—a sign of his privilege and prestige. He puts a signet ring on his finger—a mark of his father's authority and full permission to transact business on his behalf.

The father fully reinstates his son right away. No trial period to prove he's really back. No punishing him, no relegating him to some kind of family purgatory until he pays off his debt. His boy is back, and the father puts him right back where he was before he left, just like nothing ever happened!

I really hope you can see the spiritual truths about your Abba in the story. It doesn't matter what you've done. It doesn't matter how low you've sunk or how far you've wandered. It doesn't matter what stains you or how badly you stink of sin.

All that matters to Him is that you're back. That you've remembered how good His love felt and how good you had it in His house. That you've turned away from everything out there and you've come back to where the love is. He was waiting for you the whole time you were away, and when you came back to your senses, He took you back with no criticism or condemnation.

Walking in your sonship means fully embracing your Father's forgiveness and living joyfully in the abundance of His full restoration. You're not just a lowly servant who's grudgingly allowed to be in the house but not permitted to have a place at the table. You're highly esteemed and precious in His sight. You're cherished and exalted and favored.

Not because *you're* so good, but because *He* is.

Someone really needs to hear this, so listen closely—you're not on probation when you come back home. You don't have to mope around in shame and wear the dirty rags of regret for the remainder of your days. You don't have to prove yourself or work your way back into His good graces.

You can let go of the guilt!

Your Father has forgotten all about what you did. He's not holding it against you. He's not holding it over your head. It doesn't matter how bad it was. He doesn't care about what you did. He only cares about you.

Your Father's just glad to have you back. He's more than glad—He's overjoyed! He's ecstatic! And He can't wait to show you how happy He is!

Dear Abba,

I'm unspeakably grateful for your awesome and amazing love! It truly is beyond belief. It's too much to comprehend. I'm so unworthy, but you love me so deeply anyway.

I'm so glad that you know me, and that you know me so well that no amount of dirt can keep you from recognizing me. Thank you for still seeing me through my sin. Thank you for your unwavering readiness to receive me back and embrace me as your child even after everything I've done. Thank you for a love that my worst disobedience can't diminish. Thank you for full restoration.

Please help me to walk in the fullness of your forgiveness. Help me to step out of shame and guilt and embarrassment over my past. Help me to hold my head high and just walk proudly in my sonship, grateful for your amazing grace and rejoicing in your incredible love! And teach me to forgive others the way you've forgiven me. Let your heart of radical mercy and compassion be in me. I pray in Jesus' mighty name, amen!

18

Children Are Expensive!

Abba's love is amazing! Your appreciation of it will only deepen as you learn more and more about it. One astounding revelation scripture provides is that we're adopted children. Paul writes in Romans 8:15 about the Spirit of adoption within us that empowers us to cry, "Abba!"

The Greek word for "adopt" literally means to put in the place of a son. It's taking someone who's not a natural child and treating them as though they are. It's taking an outsider in and making them the full beneficiary of all the blessings and privileges of a family member.

Adoption is an *incredible* feat of love. I admire those who do it. I sometimes wonder if I could. To be honest, I'm not entirely sure. That's why I have all the respect in the world for those who do it right.

I marvel at people who possess the heart to take in someone else's children and count those children as their very own. People with the love and grace inside them to make no distinction between their biological children and those who have a stranger's blood in their veins. People who wholeheartedly welcome kids who don't look like them or talk like them or act like them, and love them unconditionally.

You and I don't look like our Father. Naturally speaking, there's not much resemblance at all. He's holy. We're not. He's all light, all the time. We gravitate toward the dark. He's perfectly good, through and through. Us, not so much.

And yet here we are, sitting comfortably at Abba's table! Accepted. Embraced. Fully a part of the family.

He lets us take His name. He gives us the privilege of calling Him Abba and calling ourselves His children. He lets us come to Him day and night to ask for whatever we need. He even writes us into His will and gives us an inheritance. That's the highest form of love—to take ungodly and ungrateful creatures like us, and to treat us like beloved, precious children, His very own offspring.

That's awesome! But it gets even better.

There's an important contrast in scripture that's worth taking note of. It's the difference between us and our "big Brother." See, we're all the Father's *adopted* sons and daughters, but Jesus is the Father's only *begotten* Son.

Think of it this way: we're all His children, but Jesus is God's only "biological child." He's the only One who's holy like the Father. He's the only One who's totally righteous and thoroughly good like the Father. He's the only One who bears a perfect family resemblance, the spitting image of God. The rest of us are adopted kids.

Now, have you ever thought about what your Father did to finalize your adoption? If not, get ready to have your mind blown. Imagine you're in the process of adopting a child. You're excited to do this and you're relieved to be taking the final steps of this long journey. You've done all the paperwork and passed all the checks. You've completed every requirement.

Then one day you get the call you've been waiting for. The person on the other end says, "Congratulations! Everything looks good. All the paperwork is in, and we're ready to go forward. There's just one last thing left to do in order to finalize the adoption—we need you to bring us your son. Once you hand him over, you can take your new baby home!"

If you're anything like me, your response would probably go something along the lines of, "Wait…what?!? You mean to tell me that in order to adopt and bless this *other* child, I've got to give up my *own* child? Yeah, that's not going to happen. I'm sorry, but it's just not."

No matter how excited you were to bring a new son or daughter into your family, everything would come to a screeching halt if that were the condition to complete it. However happy you had been to add to your brood, however badly you wanted to love this new baby, it wouldn't go any further if the price were your biological child. No way, no how. You just wouldn't do it. You *couldn't*.

But that's exactly what God the Father did!

He sacrificed His one and only biological Son to become Father to a bunch of kids who look nothing like Him. That right there is some nonsensical love! That's some totally irrational, completely illogical love! It's ridiculous and unreasonable. It doesn't make any sense, but that's exactly what your Father did to make you His child. That's how badly He had to have you and me.

Listen and listen good—don't *ever* doubt your worth!

Don't you dare entertain the enemy's lies about you, not even for one second. Whatever falsehoods that deceiver whispers in your ear, you know better now. The price your Father paid for you proves your value to Him.

No matter what anyone else thinks of you.

No matter what anyone else says about you.

No matter how anyone else treats you.

You were worth *everything* to Him, and there was nothing He wouldn't do to have you for Himself. If you're a parent, you know that feeling. You know that you would go to any lengths—even lay down your own life—to give your children a chance to live.

If you struggle with your sense of self-worth, you need to make John 3:16 the center of your renewed identity. I know, I know—we've heard that verse so many times that it's become something of a church cliché. The magnitude of its meaning has gotten lost with the repetition. But close your eyes and say it slowly and let it sink in. Let it inspire you and thrill you and liberate you all over again.

You were worth the life-blood of God's only begotten Son!

You were worth all of that purity and perfection. He laid all of that goodness, beauty, and virtue on the altar just to claim you. You were worth every bit of the undeserved agony, every last iota of the pain He endured to get you back. You were worth it all.

So start living like it.

Dear Abba,

I thank you so much for bringing me into your family! I know I don't belong, not based on my own goodness or worthiness. I know I only deserve to be on the outside looking in, but you gave me a place at your table! You chose to see an imperfect child like me the same way you see your perfect Son Jesus when you dressed me in His righteousness! I'm honored by the love you showed by adopting me, and I'm humbled by the price you paid to do it.

I pray for eyes to always see my value to you. Regardless of how I might mess up. Regardless of what the world says about me. Regardless of how I feel about myself at times. Help me to always hold on to the knowledge that I was worth the life of your only begotten Son, that you spared no expense to have me by your side! Never let the enemy cause me to doubt my importance to you, and help me to live out the value you placed on my life when you paid for it with Jesus' blood. In His marvelous name, amen!

19

What Do You Mean, "If"?

Sometimes you can gauge the value of a thing by how badly someone else doesn't want you to have it. Even if they can't claim it for themselves, they'll be content with keeping it away from you.

"If I can't have it, then no one can."

Some have called this the "dog in the manger" complex. The dog doesn't eat the grain, but he won't let the oxen eat it either. He harasses and hounds them and keeps them away from the feeding trough. Jesus said the Pharisees had this twisted spirit and didn't even realize it. He told them that they didn't enter the kingdom themselves, and they wouldn't let anyone else go in either (Matthew 23:13).

Your relationship with the Father is the most important thing you have. It is supremely valuable—nothing else even compares. It's *everything*. And, ironically enough, it was the devil himself who proved it! When he made our fellowship with God his main target, he proved how spiritually significant it really is.

See, the enemy deeply resents the loving relationship God has with His children. He *hates* you more than anything because he knows that God *loves* you more than anything. So destroying that relationship is his highest priority.

If he can't have it, no one else will.

Go back to Luke 4 and revisit Satan's temptation of the Lord in the wilderness. Notice that two of the three tests began with a challenge to Jesus' sense of security in the Father. Twice he said, "If you are the Son of God..." (You can almost hear the jealousy dripping from his lips!)

Take note that it wasn't Jesus' power that Satan called into question. It wasn't His holiness or His knowledge of scripture that was being challenged. It was His *sonship*. The devil was trying to make Jesus doubt His relationship with the Father.

The word "devil," by the way, means "accuser." He's a slanderer. He seeks to disrupt and divide through disparaging words. He loves using smear tactics to turn people against each other. Satan's an expert at subtle insinuation, very craftily planting unnoticeable seeds of doubt. In fact, this was the very first trick he ever used on humankind.

Think about it. First, he asked Eve if God really said not to eat the fruit. Then he told her that the reason God forbade it was because it would make them like Him. Now, did you catch what he was *really* saying? The subtle suggestion was that God wasn't telling them the whole story, that He was somehow keeping them in the dark. Satan was insinuating that the Lord had given them *some* things, but He was keeping the best stuff for Himself.

The accuser was accusing the Father of holding out on His children. And the solution he offered was that, if God wouldn't give it, then they'd have to take it for themselves.

So when the devil came to Christ in the wilderness, he was recycling the same old trick. He was trying to convince the Son that the Father didn't really love Him like He thought He did. In a season of hunger and need, he wanted Jesus to question the reality of that connection. The devil wanted to get Jesus to a place of doubt because he knew that, just as it had done in the garden so long ago, doubt leads to desperation.

And desperation leads to disaster.

A lot of people get in and stay in unhealthy relationships trying to get something the devil convinced them God either couldn't or wouldn't give them. So many yearning, seeking people settle on addictive and destructive habits trying to find some satisfaction, *anything* to fill the emptiness they're experiencing. If the enemy can make you feel like you're missing out on something, then he can entice you to scratch your "God itch" in ungodly ways.

The kicker is that Satan was actually selling Eve something she already had. The devil said that if they ate the fruit, they'd be like God—but they already were! They were made in the image and likeness of God; they already had divine DNA.

But if the enemy can saddle you with what I call a Satanic sense of insufficiency—a false feeling that you're not good enough, pretty enough, smart enough, strong enough, rich enough, or whatever enough—then he can get you to bite on the destructive delights that he's dangling in front of you.

And it's all downhill from there.

That's why you need to know how important your relationship with God is. That's why you need to hold on to how valuable you are to Him, why you need to cling so tightly to the knowledge of how much the Father truly and deeply loves you as His child. When you know who you are to your Father and what you have in Him, no lesser substitute for His presence and power in your life will ever suffice.

Acceptance? No thanks. I'm already fully embraced—flaws and all—by Someone far greater than anyone else I'd like to like me. So if I have to be someone other than who He wants me to be to get it, their acceptance isn't worth it.

Validation? I'm good. I'm already wrapped in the righteousness of the only begotten Son. My Father gives me purpose. He listens to my voice. He confirms when I'm right and corrects when I'm wrong. So I don't need to lower myself for "likes" from the world or get people's approval of the path that I'm on.

Pleasure? Pass. I'm already high on His favor and basking in His blessings on my life, blessings that I'm still discovering every day. I have joy beyond measure and peace that passes understanding, so there's no artificial high or fleeting carnal gratification that I need to make me feel like life is worth living.

There's nothing Satan can sell you when you realize you've already got it all.

One little word can do a whole lot of damage. "If" is one of those words. It stirs up a sense of uncertainty. (Just a minute ago, you were *sure* that you were sure, but now...you're not so sure.) It creates suspicion and instigates mistrust. It makes you hesitate and hold back.

Don't let the devil do that to you. When it comes to being a child of your heavenly Father, there are no ifs, ands, or buts about it.

Dear Abba,

I thank you for exposing the enemy's intentions and opening my eyes to what is most valuable. I pray today for the clarity to always see how much you care about me as your child. Protect me from any and all destructive doubts. Never let me question my connection with you. I pray that, even in the wilderness seasons of my life, I'll be just as steadfast in my sonship as Jesus was. Let me be so firmly rooted in your truth about who I am that no lie of the enemy can ever shake my faith in your unconditional love.

I pray that I will always find my fulfillment in you. When I'm hungry, be my food. When I'm thirsty, be my drink. When I'm cold, be my shelter. Teach me to be joyfully content with who you are and what you give. Grant me such a strong spirit of satisfaction with you that nothing of this world could ever take your place at the center of my life. In the awesome name of Jesus, amen!

20

The Apple of His Eye

This book is really for believers. I certainly do hope it helps someone come to faith in God. That would be wonderful, but that's not my main intent in writing it. What I'm really aiming for is to help those of us who already know God to go deeper in our relationships with Him and hold on just a little tighter to what we have.

See, that's the key word—relationship. It's all about your walk with Him. A deeply fulfilling walk. A walk that brings you comfort and security. One that fills your life with purpose and meaning and joy.

As we near the end of this journey, let's go back to the beginning one more time. We saw God walking with man in the garden. It was a beautiful picture of love, but there was something ugly hiding at the fringes. There was someone lurking in the shadows, looking on this relationship with resentment. Already hateful of God, the devil soon became hateful of what God loved most—us.

Satan quickly came to despise the fellowship that God cherished with His creation, a fellowship that he himself could no longer enjoy. So with carefully crafted lies and well-disguised motivations, he duped us into walking away from the One who walked with us. He made it his mission to pull us apart, and he's been at it ever since.

Even when God's goodness catches up to us and brings us back to our senses, the enemy still tries to keep us at arm's length from the Father's fullness. He tries to burden us with the same sense of shame that had the prodigal son crawling back and begging to simply be a servant. See, the devil has no problem with settling for small degrees of destruction. He's totally good with slow erosion instead of sudden eradication.

If he can't keep you from knowing God, he's content to keep you from knowing everything you need to know *about* God.

That's why the devil loves religion. He revels in the ritualistic. He delights in the dull practice of formulaic routines and the mindless adherence to empty traditions. He's totally cool with "church," as long as you just keep *going* and never start *being*. To put it simply, if Satan had to pick, he'd much rather you only see yourself as a servant of God than to realize that you're actually a son!

The spirit of servanthood will have you focused on *performance*. It keeps you wondering whether or not you've done enough good to outweigh your bad. It keeps you questioning your place in the house, doubtful that you really deserve it and fearful that, at any moment, someone better will come along and take it from you. It keeps you languishing under the dread of the lash, always anxious about being judged and punished.

The spirit of servanthood keeps you working *for* your master's love, constantly trying to prove yourself to a disdainful and disapproving lord. And if he can keep you there, the enemy knows there's a real good chance that you'll become so disappointed and disillusioned that you walk away all over again.

On the other hand, the spirit of sonship will have you focused on *position* instead of performance. It's not about what you have or haven't done—it's about who you are in relation to your Father. It's about where His love has placed you despite where you deserve to be. The spirit of sonship keeps you walking confidently in His grace, even when your own goodness doesn't measure up. It keeps you moving securely in the knowledge that you can't lose your Father's love and that your place at His table is yours and yours alone, as long as you choose to fill it.

The spirit of sonship keeps you living under the peaceful assurance that, even though there may be *consequences* for your sin, there's no *condemnation* in the only begotten Son, whose righteousness you now wear. It keeps you working *from* the Father's love, not feeling like you need to earn it, but simply loving Him for loving you so much.

The spirit of servanthood will have you swinging between two very dangerous extremes: self-condemnation and self-exaltation. In other words, if it's all about your performance as a servant, then when you fail and fall short, you go to a place of depression and defeat, feeling worthless and unlovable. Or when you're doing well (or *think* you're doing well), then your head swells and your nose turns up in the air. Pride sets in and, well, you know what comes next.

The spirit of sonship keeps you level and balanced. When you know who you are to your Father, your faults and failures never get you so low that you want to walk away or give up on yourself. You know that He loves you unconditionally and that you can't lose that love. Knowing that He doesn't condemn you keeps you from condemning yourself. And on the other hand, you can't get puffed up because you know that everything good you've got and everything good you do is by the Father's grace. It's His blood in your veins, His food in your belly, His clothes on your back, and His roof over your head!

So you've got to decide who you're going to be—a servant or a son. One is a role to be played; the other is a relationship to be savored. One eventually becomes a burden, while the other is only ever a blessing.

Who you decide to be is going to be determined by how you decide to see your God. I hope that this book has begun to help you see Him as much more than a Master. He's so much more than a King or a Lord. He's a Father. He's a Dad. That's what He's always wanted to be. You can call Him Abba.

And when you get that in your spirit, you'll know that you're the apple of His eye. You'll know that you are His heart. You're His beloved, precious child.

You are your Papa's pride and joy.

Dear Abba,

I'm so blessed to be your child and I'm so glad to have you as my Father! Thank you for all you've done to make someone like me a part of your family and to bring me into relationship with you. I don't deserve your presence in my life, but I'm so thankful for your grace that gives it anyway.

I pray that your Spirit will lead me into an ever-deepening understanding of what my sonship truly means. Help me to embrace the fullness of a close, personal relationship with you and to experience all the joy and comfort that comes with being your child.

Help me to move beyond seeing myself as just a servant. Teach me to walk in complete confidence in your love for me. Teach me to move with absolute assurance that I'm yours and you're mine. Free me from all doubt and fear. Remove from my heart every inclination toward feeling like I have to prove my worth or earn your acceptance, and let me just rest in your unconditional love for me as your child. I pray for perfect peace and total security in the spirit of sonship. In Jesus' name, amen!

Printed in the United States
By Bookmasters